D0628738

"The best and most beautiful things
in the world cannot be seen nor touched...
but are felt in the heart."

- Helen Keller

Popping the Question, Seattle Style

Seattle Style

99 Real-Life Proposals from the Pacific Northwest

By Emerson Robbins
Editor: Alicia M. Lawver

ericson dorow, inc

Popping the Question, Seattle Style:
99 Real-Life Proposals from the Pacific Northwest

Copyright © 2006 E. E. Robbins, LLC

All rights reserved. No portion of this book may be
reproduced or utilized in any form, or by electronic
or other means, without the prior written permission
of E. E. Robbins, LLC.

First edition
Printed in Canada

By Emerson Robbins

Editor: Alicia M. Lawver
Project Manager: Jody Ericson Dorow
Copy Editor: Judy Gouldthorpe
Book and Cover Design: Nancy Gellos
Cover Art: Erik Hall

ISBN 0-9787891-0-5   978-0-9787891-0-7

Photo: Bryan Myss

Introduction

"*L*ove makes the world go 'round," they say. Well, I don't know if it's true, but I do know that sharing your life with someone you love sure makes the ride more fun. My wife, Sherri, never fails to keep me laughing and loving.

I've had the rare privilege of being in the engagement ring business for the past 20-some years, and I've heard lots of remarkable proposal stories. What I've learned from this experience is that how one proposes is even more important than the ring one proposes with. Both should last a lifetime — the ring and the cherished memories of that moment when he (or she) popped the question.

So I decided it was finally time to put all these wonderfully creative and romantic stories into a book. The purpose of this book is not to become a best seller, but rather to help guys (or ladies) realize that when you "pop the question," it may be the most important question you will ever ask anyone. How you ask that question will be remembered and, we hope, cherished for as long as you both live. It may even become a story retold by your children and grandchildren.

So that is what our book is all about: 99 real-life proposal stories to help inspire others to make their proposal their own, to make it creative and romantic — a memory to be treasured forever.

We dedicate this book to all those who live and love in our beautiful Pacific Northwest, where the skies are often gray, but romance keeps our hearts warm.

Emerson Robbins

The Alpine Proposal

Stephen and Susan

*S*tephen and Susan had spent most of their time dating exploring the wilderness, so his romantic plans included signing them up for a mountaineering course in Canada. As they packed, Stephen tucked away a special piece of "equipment" in his backpack — a carabiner engraved with the phrase "Will you marry me?" — and his great-great-grandmother's diamond, set in a new ring.

Arriving in Canmore, Alberta, the couple met with their team, donned 70-pound packs and headed out on a "moderate" hike. For six hours, they climbed a nearly vertical trail to an alpine base camp. Within a short hike of the camp was an endless vista of glaciers and craggy peaks. It was in this amazing landscape that the group hung in crevasses, practiced rescues, ice climbed, and learned how to pull themselves out of icy canyons. Susan was having a great time, and had no idea what was in store.

The last morning in the mountains, the teams got together at the base of a glacier and roped up for a summit attempt. Stephen had pre-arranged to have Susan on his team, and in the line directly behind him. They trekked through snowstorms, whiteouts and numerous crevasse fields. As their team neared the summit, the guide stopped to take a "group photo." That was Stephen's cue. He found his special carabiner and carefully sent it down the rope with the ring dangling.

Susan's reaction said it all. By the time Stephen had climbed down to her and gotten on one knee, she was crying. He slid the glove off and the ring on. And the rest of the team cheered as the couple gained the summit and the proposal was recorded in the logbook on top of Mount Gordon.

Bed-and-Breakfast and Briquettes

Wade and Jada

Wade and Jada were celebrating their one-year dating anniversary and Wade's birthday with a weekend at Run of the River, a romantic bed-and-breakfast. But Wade had ulterior motives. That night while Jada slept, he crept out of the room for about two hours.

The next morning, after they'd gotten ready for breakfast, Wade suggested that they take a peek at their view. He opened the curtains, and down below their balcony, written in the snow with about 40 pounds of charcoal briquettes, were the words "Jada, Will U Marry Me?"

"He then pulled out a beautiful ring," Jada said, "and told me wonderful things. I said YES before he even finished."

Fire Ladder

Patrick and Callie

*P*atrick and Callie arrived for dinner at the historic Cloud Room in Seattle one evening to meet up with friends who were in town visiting, or so she was told. After being seated for a while at a lovely view table, Callie heard a fire engine's siren. Looking over the balcony near their table, she saw a fire truck's ladder extending up the side of the nearby Paramount Theatre, and then toward the restaurant where they were eating.

Callie began to panic, thinking that the building was on fire. She didn't notice the cameras going off around her. When the fire truck's ladder was fully extended (seven stories), the firefighter on the end of the ladder unrolled a huge sign that read: "Callie, I love you. Will you marry me?" Callie's knees buckled, and she fell to the floor. She landed in front of Patrick, a firefighter, who was on one knee with a ring. "The one thing in my life that I have never questioned is that I want to marry you," said Patrick. "Will you be my wife?"

As Callie looked around to see if this was really happening, she noticed a crowd of friends on the street clapping, nearby apartment dwellers clapping, and people on the patio and in the lounge clapping. The server came over with champagne and flowers, and then Callie noticed all the cameras. Patrick had planned everything. "It was so romantic, so spectacular, and the details this man put into planning were amazing," said Callie. "I felt like the most beautiful and loved woman in the world."

The Commercial

Joe and Kerri

Joe, a copywriter for a large ad agency, worked hard to compose a personal yet quirky proposal by writing a "commercial" for a jewelry company based on the details of how Kerri and he met and fell in love. It had funny stuff. It had romantic stuff. And it definitely had personal stuff. Joe even persuaded the jewelry company's voice-over talent to record a fake ad spot, which he put onto a CD.

Fast-forward to a week later: Joe picked Kerri up from work and they headed to a party, or so she was told. As they neared their destination, Joe casually "changed" the radio station, and his personalized commercial started playing. Because he had written it in exactly the same style as the real radio spots, Kerri didn't immediately notice anything different. Joe's pseudo-commercial started with a line he knew would hit a nerve: "Does it sometimes feel like everyone you know is getting engaged?" On cue, Kerri looked over at Joe and shook her head in frustration, then stared out the window. Then it got more personal.

"You two probably met at work, didn't you?"

"You couldn't take your eyes off his rippling biceps . . ."

As other parts of their story began to unfold, Kerri started screaming, "You're doing it! You're finally doing it!" Joe took Kerri to a nearby arboretum, where they walked up a candlelit path to a clearing. He had already set up a small table with a bottle of wine and more candles. No longer need Kerri wait. Joe got down on his knees and asked the question she longed to hear.

Lady and the Tramp

Mark and Betty

*M*ark and Betty's romance was well marinated in plenty of love notes and poetry attached to homemade meatballs that Mark made for her. His overtures, reminiscent of the childhood love story *Lady and the Tramp*, hit the right notes with Betty. Soon the meatballs were their "theme."

So when Mark decided to propose, he had obvious material to draw from. He invited Betty over for a spaghetti-and-meatball dinner — and made her a "special" meatball. As Betty cut into her artfully crafted dinner, she discovered more than spices. Upon seeing the ring, she didn't have to wait to hear the words.

Dolphin Delivery

George and Brandy

A friend's destination wedding was George's answer to how to pop the question. Brandy's love of dolphins and a trip to Hawaii played perfectly into his plans. He told Brandy that his uncle, who lived in Honolulu, had bought them tickets to swim with the dolphins. What Brandy didn't know was that George had spent weeks working with the resort to plan a proposal not to be forgotten.

Upon arrival at the dolphin resort, George slipped a special something to one dolphin trainer while another distracted Brandy with pictures of the dolphins. At the end of the show, the trainers announced that there was one more activity and asked George and Brandy to get in the water. The trainer explained that since the couple had been giving the dolphins fish all day, they wanted to give Brandy a thank-you gift. One of the trainers then threw a large floating box into the water and signaled the dolphin to retrieve it.

As Brandy opened the box that the dolphin brought her, she was shocked to see that the inside was designed like a regular jewelry box, with an exquisite ring sitting in the center. George took the ring, asked his question, and the dolphin did flips as George placed the ring on Brandy's finger.

Falling for Him

Luke and Karen

*K*aren thought skydiving would be a big enough way to celebrate her 30th birthday. Apparently her boyfriend thought differently. Dressed in jumpsuits, padded helmets and goggles, Luke and Karen readied themselves to jump. The airplane doors flew open and Karen's heart skipped a beat. Excitement, exhilaration, fear and love: it was all there. As Luke stood on the launch pad and braced himself for the leap, he said . . . something. At 8,000 feet, with the sound of the twin-prop plane rumbling through their bodies, his words were drowned out. And then Luke was gone. It was her turn.

Karen quickly followed Luke into an "amazing" free fall. Before she knew it, her parachute was open and she was gliding toward the ground. Her instructor began to point out the incredible views, including a large sign placed next to their intended landing spot. Karen's level of exhilaration surpassed that of the free fall as she read "Will You Marry Me, Karen?"

She landed safely, and Luke approached her with what she described as "those adoring Karen eyes." Struggling to get out of her parachute, she shouted with joy and blew him kisses. Then Luke dropped to his knees and repeated his earlier question. Her response? "Yes, yes, yes!" They then enjoyed their first "engaged couple" kiss and toasted with the champagne and strawberries that Luke had waiting.

♥

A Hike for Her Hand

Patrick and Marcy

*P*atrick knew that the ring he had created for Marcy would get a yes. He had worked hard to find the perfect band, the perfect stone. He had even customized the ring's head to resemble a tulip, Marcy's favorite flower. But he wanted the proposal to be just as memorable. The couple's first date had been skiing on Crystal Mountain. The first time they said "I love you" was in the mountains of British Columbia, and they'd made three trips to Whistler. So he looked to the mountains for inspiration.

Marcy, an avid hiker, was delighted when Patrick suggested they try out the Naches Peak hike in Mount Rainier National Park, which unbeknownst to her was just a few miles from the location of their first date. The day of the hike brought blue skies and temperatures in the 70s, rolling meadows full of wildflowers and stunning views of the Cascades. When they unexpectedly came upon a mountain lake, Patrick knew he had found the perfect place.

He reached into his backpack and produced a picnic blanket. His heart was pounding as they snacked on fresh strawberries. Then Patrick pulled out his iPod and some small speakers. Their song, "True Companion" by Mark Cohn, began to play. And Patrick got down on one knee as he asked Marcy to spend the rest of her life with him.

Engagement Raft

Joe and Allison

*J*oe invited Allison to go kayaking that day, and so off they went. About a half mile from shore, Allison spotted a lone raft drifting in the current. As they approached, she could see that it was decorated with beautiful white silk netting and a candlelit table for two. The couple docked their kayak with the romantic free-floating raft and boarded.

Allison was wide-eyed and giddy with excitement, and Joe was glad. He had spent two entire days preparing and decorating the raft. It was carpeted in turf, with six-foot posts in the four corners holding the white silk overhead. Tiny white lanterns with tea candles bathed them both in a soft glow. The table held a candlelit floral centerpiece. They sat down, and Joe explained that he wanted to celebrate her recent accomplishments and her return to graduate school. He reached beneath the table and brought out Allison's favorite wine, some gourmet cheese, bread, and oil and balsamic vinegar for dipping.

As the raft floated down Hood Canal and the sun began to set, Joe presented Allison with what he called "a silly little gift" and handed her a wooden box. She used a small key to open the box and discovered a dried flower bouquet, the same one she'd caught just a week before at her friend's wedding. At that point, Joe pulled his great-grandmother's ring from his pocket and asked her to marry him. Through happy tears, Allison said yes as Joe slipped the ring on her finger. Then he took out his journal from three years earlier. Only a few days after they began dating, Joe had written that he'd met the woman he was going to marry.

Mariner Moose

Paul and Maria

*T*hree years after Paul and Maria's first date — a late September Mariners/Rangers game — the happy couple sat in Section 142, Row 15, at Safeco Field with Paul's sister and brother-in-law. It was a beautiful evening, a night like many others they'd enjoyed together at the baseball field. But tonight was different. Paul had a special pitch saved for later in the game.

Maria left her seat a few times during the game for trips to the concourse, causing some anxious moments for Paul. Eventually, however, as all four of the group relaxed in their seats, the Mariners' mascot (the Mariner Moose) appeared in the aisle. Paul looked up and asked, "Are you ready, Moose?" The six-foot mute mountain of fur responded with a big nod and then held up a large sign that read: "Maria, Will You Marry Paul?" Paul got down on one knee and presented Maria with the ring. And both Paul and the Moose got kissed that night.

♥

Cracker Jack

Rod and Melanie

Rod was a penniless student when he proposed, so his intended not only didn't expect a ring, but she didn't suspect a thing when she dug the prize out of her Cracker Jack that day. "Now we can get engaged," Melanie joked before she realized that the ring in her caramel-coated popcorn was real. Rod had taken a box of Cracker Jack and very carefully unsealed the bottom, removing the popcorn and the prize. Slicing one side of the paper prize, he had inserted an engagement ring and then carefully reassembled the box. He even resealed the bottom with candle wax.

Once Melanie realized that this was no penny prize she was holding, Rod quickly proposed and received the answer he was looking for. The couple now celebrates with Cracker Jack every Valentine's Day — and Melanie is always eager to see her prize.

A Few of Her Favorite Things

Ben and Addie

*B*en decided to add a sentimental touch to his proposal by re-creating Addie's favorite date. They began their evening reminiscing over a couple of beers on the Seattle waterfront while waiting for a ferry. When they reached the nearby island, the couple walked to a little Mexican restaurant. Everything was perfect: the view, the weather, the company. As they headed back to the ferry, Ben took Addie on a detour along the waterfront, and they ended up sitting on the same bench they had used during "Addie's favorite date."

Ben suggested that they "borrow" one of the rowboats. Addie felt a little mischievous as they rowed out into the harbor, hoping the owner wouldn't come looking for his boat and find it missing. (She later learned that the boat belonged to a friend of Ben's.) As she gazed at the Seattle skyline, all lit up, she began to hear music — one of their favorite songs. They followed the music and rowed up to a large sailboat, which Addie eventually recognized as belonging to a friend of theirs. They boarded the boat, and Addie discovered a table with wine, candles and roses.

Ben's guitar was also waiting, and he began to play a song he had written for her. Halfway through the song, Ben stopped, told Addie all the things he loved about her and then asked her to marry him. Addie said yes as Ben finished his song.

Avian Intentions

Mark and Lindsay

*M*ark wanted to propose to Lindsay in a grand and majestic way. He wanted to get her to a mountaintop, he wanted to get down on one knee, and he wanted to have a trained falcon land on his arm with the ring attached to its leg. And he tried — oh did he try — to make that happen.

First, Mark tracked down a falconer and spent many sessions training an Arctic falcon named Bianca to land on his arm. Hours and hours he practiced until he got the bird to come to him. But then there was the problem of trying to get Lindsay to go on a hike with him. He bought her new boots, he scheduled it time and time again, but no luck. He even asked a friend of Lindsay's to persuade her to go on a hike, a shorter hike than his original grand ambitions. But no, Lindsay wanted to do laundry.

Enough was enough. One day when he was visiting Lindsay, she noticed that Mark wasn't acting like himself. When she asked what was up, Mark was quite honest and came clean about his field trips and his "affair" with Bianca the bird. Lindsay then asked if he had the ring with him, and he said, "No, it's hidden." She ran off to scour the house, and turned up an empty box. With the empty box in hand, she knew where to go. Mark had hidden the ring in one of her grandmother's antique collectible pillboxes (which had great sentimental meaning for her). After Lindsay had gone through a couple of pillboxes, Mark grabbed the one with the hidden treasure and didn't make her wait any longer.

Family Flyby

*J*osh and Stephanie had been planning a road trip. Or at least that's what Stephanie thought. The morning of their planned departure, Josh arranged for Stephanie's best friend to take her for a girls' day out while he sneaked off to the airport to pick up his family, who had flown in from Reno. (Stephanie's family was local.) When Stephanie returned home, Josh suggested that they leave in the morning instead. She agreed, and they headed downtown for a night out. Stephanie had no idea that Josh had secret plans until he pulled into a parking lot — and led her onto a seaplane.

After the standard aerial tour of Puget Sound, the pilot took them lower to get a closer view of the beach. As the plane skimmed the water, Josh told Stephanie to look out his window. She did, and her eyes filled with tears when she saw her siblings, aunts, uncles, cousins and grandmother cheering on the beach as they held a 40-foot banner that read, "Steph, will you marry me?" When she looked back at Josh, he held up the ring and — over the loud plane engines — asked her to be his wife.

When they landed, Josh's family and Stephanie's parents and best friend were waiting with flowers and hugs. They all piled into a limo and drove back to the beach, where they celebrated their engagement alongside loved ones with a champagne toast.

Spell the Coffee

Jason and Leslie

Leslie grew up in Washington State, and she never lost the craving for that popular Seattle scene: Starbucks. For Leslie and her family, Starbucks was an essential part of their daily routine.

When Leslie and Jason started dating, he wasn't a coffee fan. And he understandably thought that Leslie's family was obsessed. But Leslie knew that Jason had a sweet tooth, and she used that weakness to tempt him with Starbucks' specialty drinks. Her plan worked, and she no longer had to drag him to her favorite spot.

So after a lovely yet uneventful dinner, Leslie wasn't even remotely suspicious when Jason suggested that they head over to their local Starbucks. As usual, the couple took along a travel version of Scrabble, a favorite pastime. After they had ordered, Jason asked Leslie to wait for their drinks while he grabbed a table and set up the Scrabble game.

When Leslie brought the drinks to the table, she noticed that Jason was watching her, and that there were already letters on the board. So she looked down and read the letters, which spelled out "WILL YOU MARRY ME." Surprised and speechless, Leslie looked up at Jason as he pulled out a ring.

"I just stared at him for a second," she remembered. Then, realizing that he hadn't left her those three little Scrabble letters to answer with, she responded with a hearty "Yes!"

Lights on the Water

Keith and Christine

One night, Keith came home and excitedly told Christine he'd gotten an important job interview. To celebrate, he'd made reservations at the Edgewater Hotel, the couple's "special place." Christine couldn't understand why they were going to spend so much money simply because Keith had gotten an interview, but she went along with it.

When they arrived at the hotel, there were chocolate-covered strawberries and champagne in their room, and the couple relaxed for a while. At six o'clock, they went for dinner at the restaurant and were seated at a view table in front of some sliding glass doors. Dinner came and went, and so did dessert. Keith commented on how close the boat outside was to the dock. Christine had thought nothing of it, and didn't look.

Then the manager came in from outside and opened the doors by their table. At first, all Christine could think was "It's freezing out there! How rude!" She was about to reach for her coat when she noticed something shining to her left. Soon it came into full view: "Christine, will you marry me?" was written in Christmas lights on an 18-foot-long, 4-foot-high sign on the side of a boat. Keith got down on one knee and proposed. Christine accepted. And they both cried as the entire restaurant applauded and their parents appeared and joined the happy couple.

"It was the most romantic and thoughtful proposal ever," remembered Christine.

Slippery Salmon

Jeff and Jenelle

While strolling through Seattle's Pike Place Market with Jenelle and his two teenage daughters, Jeff said he needed to find a restroom, a cue for his daughters to keep Jenelle occupied while he initiated "the plan." Jeff then ran over to the Fish Market, where the employees are famous for tossing around 30-pound salmon and harassing passersby with their antics. He pulled out an engagement ring — enclosed in a crushed-velvet box and a small zipper-lock bag — and asked the manager for a little assistance. The manager cheerfully agreed, and they placed the ring inside the mouth of a very large salmon and hid the fish behind the counter.

Jeff returned to Jenelle and his daughters, and they decided on fresh salmon for dinner. They returned to the Fish Market and asked for a salmon. The guys behind the counter immediately started yelling and grabbed Jenelle, pulling her behind the counter and putting one of their fish aprons around her embarrassed neck.

The designated salmon was then thrown 20 feet through the air and over the counter to Jenelle, who caught it with the assistance of one of the pros. On cue, the engagement ring flew out of the fish's mouth. Jenelle was a bit confused as to what had just popped out of her dinner's mouth. The Fish Guy held up the ring box for the gathered crowd to see and then presented it to her. Jeff joined her behind the counter, grabbed the ring, and removed the plastic bag before kneeling down to ask the love of his life to marry him — while the crowd cheered.

Caution: Marriage Proposal Ahead

Chris and Maria

*D*ressed in steel-toed boots, an orange safety vest and a hard hat borrowed from her construction-worker brother, Maria stood on the side of a four-lane road and waited. She'd arranged to meet her boyfriend for lunch. On the route she knew he'd be driving, Maria set up a stand with a bright orange sign that read: "Caution: Marriage Proposal Ahead." The handheld stop sign that Maria gripped had also been altered, and read, "Chris, Marry Me?"

Many people noticed Maria and her sign. But not Chris. He drove blithely past and turned in to the parking lot of the restaurant where they'd planned to meet. Then he must have done a double take, because he turned around and drove back. Maria was still wearing that construction helmet when she got down on one knee and presented him with a gold ring.

"He's obeyed all the laws of marriage," Maria said, "so I suppose it's okay if he ran that one stop sign."

Sea Slate

Eric and Julie

*I*t was a sunny Labor Day weekend, and Eric and Julie decided that it was a perfect time to spend a weekend boating and scuba diving. Several of their friends and family joined them, resulting in an eight-boat flotilla anchored in a cove.

The couple submerged to 25 feet to explore the walls of a nearby island and peruse the sea life. After about 15 minutes, Julie followed Eric around a rock corner. She tapped him on the shoulder, and he turned around and handed her his underwater slate, which read: "Julie, will you marry me?"

Taking her time before answering, Julie turned the slate over and wrote "Ring?"

Eric had that one covered. He took off his dive glove, cut a string that was securing Julie's engagement ring to the palm of his hand, and placed the ring on her finger.

Rotation Notation

Donald and Nicole

$\mathcal{T}$he week after Nicole's birthday, Donald kept telling her that she still had a surprise coming. So when he took her to the restaurant at the top of the Space Needle, she figured that was the surprise. But Donald wasn't done. "People who eat there like to make little notes on coasters or sugar packets and put them on the wall ledge, so that as the place rotates, it passes everyone sitting by the window," he said. "We always loved eating there and reading all the notes and poking fun at them."

Halfway through dinner, Donald excused himself to go to the bathroom, and on the way back he came from the opposite direction so Nicole wouldn't see him. He had several prewritten notes in his pocket so he could quickly implement his surprise. He squeezed in — politely — between some people eating several tables away from where he and Nicole were seated and set the notes on the ledge before returning to his table. Then he waited.

Soon enough, the planted notes made their way around and naturally caught their attention. At first, Nicole was stunned to see her name. Then she focused on what the rest were saying and burst into laughter. "She had always told me that a proposal should be a little cheesy yet meaningful at the same time," said Donald. "I think that captured her wishes pretty well."

Spam

John and Kara

$\mathcal{J}$ohn's proposal came in the form of Spam (the chopped meat in a can, not the annoying, obtrusive e-mails). It was at the fun, weird, now-defunct Spam-Carving Contest, a Seattle tradition. After being frequent attendees at the event, John and Kara finally decided to participate. And while this Fat Tuesday celebration no longer occurs, Kara will never forget her then-boyfriend's entry. His canned-meat carving? "MARRY ME KC."

The sponsors loved it. The judges loved it. Kara loved it. And while the carving got no award, "it was one of the coolest things ever," she said. And it did get a write-up in the local paper. Perhaps more important, it got a yes from Kara.

From Nightmares to Dreams Come True

Jason and Jen

*J*ason and Jen were attending a wedding one evening when she told him a story about the time she received some groom's cake at a wedding when she was six years old. Her mother said that if she put it under her pillow, she would dream about the person she would marry. That night, she dreamed of Dracula. All freaked out, she tried it again the next night, with the same result.

So when the "big day" drew near, Jason couldn't resist the obvious. On Halloween, he set up a scavenger hunt around town for her. The adventure started off with Jen coming home to a new outfit, a trick-or-treat bucket, a note telling her she was on a scavenger hunt, and her first clue. The hunt had her "trick-or-treating" at friends' houses — the treats including everything from lipstick that went with her outfit to more private mementos. The 10 different stops took three hours.

At the second-to-last stop, the treat was a key. The final clue was to go to "Dracula's house," which was actually Jason's house. He had decorated it to look spooky and was dressed as Dracula, with his hair slicked back and fangs in his mouth. When Jen arrived, he gave her a little pumpkin with the ultimate treat inside — a sparkling diamond engagement ring.

February 21, 2004

Bobblehead

After four months of proposal planning, R.K. had left no detail unturned. He was prepared. He was ready. He was looking for an answer.

> The time: Kimberly's birthday
> The place: a lovely restaurant
> The scene: surrounded by loved ones

Sitting at the restaurant table with her pile of presents, Kimberly opened the gift her boyfriend had painstakingly prepared for her. She burst into laughter as she peered into the box at a bobblehead doll custom-made to look exactly like her. Her hair. Her eyes. Even her outfit. Then Kimberly looked more closely and noticed a glimmer of light on the doll's left ring finger. She turned to her boyfriend with a look of confusion. But before she could speak, R.K. was on his knees with the answer, in the form of a question.

The Gas Station

Kyle and Tina

*K*yle's plan was to whisk Tina off to the San Juan Islands for a relaxing weekend at a Friday Harbor bed-and-breakfast, then propose over a romantic dinner at the Duck Soup Inn. He had no problem persuading Tina to get out of town for the weekend, but when they arrived at the restaurant, there was a large wedding party already having dinner. A good plan; the wrong moment. So after dinner, in search of a quiet, romantic spot, Kyle led Tina into the nearby woods. But "the perfect moment" remained elusive.

As the sun began to set, he suggested a walk on the beach. They soon came upon two piers, one crowded and one not. Kyle led Tina onto the empty one, which eventually brought them to a small, secluded bench.

"I knew this was it!" said Kyle. "I dropped to one knee and told her that I felt so lucky to be with her every day, that I loved her more than I could say, and that I wanted to spend the rest of my life with her." And then he asked Tina to marry him.

While on the ferry heading home the next day, the newly engaged couple looked back at the pier where Kyle had proposed — and discovered why they had been all alone. Their special spot was behind a gas station on a pier for boats. "Now my lovely wife always jokes that I proposed behind a gas station. How romantic!"

Flying by the Space Needle

Henry and Kathleen

Kathleen had just finished at the Police Academy, and Henry had planned a romantic dinner at the Space Needle's rotating restaurant to celebrate. It was also prom night, so the restaurant was packed with teens in tuxes and gowns as the couple joined the partygoers' frenzy. During appetizers, Henry pretended to chip his tooth and excused himself, actually sneaking off to enlist the host's help in videotaping the real reason why he'd brought Kathleen to the Space Needle.

As she waited for Henry to return, Kathleen noticed that the prom attendees weren't as focused on their dates anymore. The twittering had taken on a different form, and she heard whispers of "Who's Kathleen? Did she say yes?" Then Kathleen saw what they were gossiping about. An airplane flew by the Space Needle's high-altitude restaurant trailing a banner that read: "Kathleen. Marry me. Henry." The teenagers were talking about *her*.

Kathleen whipped her head around in search of Henry, and there he was — on one knee with a ring. Without hesitation, she quickly answered, "Yes, oh yes!" The couple spent the rest of their evening happily responding to notes stuck to the windows of the rotating restaurant asking, "Did you say yes?"

They were married one year later, to the day.

Her Boyfriend's a Bum

Tim and Jenny

$\mathcal{D}$inner reservations — it seemed like an ordinary way to celebrate their first anniversary, so Jenny had no reason to suspect that Tim was up to anything. He was going hunting that morning, so Jenny made plans to meet her parents at Pike Place Market to hang out and have lunch at a local crepe place.

While meandering along the Seattle waterfront with her parents, Jenny noticed a homeless man near the fountain. She thought it was odd that the man was holding a sign that read: "Homeless. Hungry. Will Marry 4 Food." Suddenly, he approached her dad and said, "Sir, I see you have two ladies. May I have one of them?"

Jenny tried to back away, thinking it was a bit weird that her parents were so calm. Her dad responded, "Well, that's my wife. But you can have my daughter; her boyfriend's a bum."

Then Jenny's dad shoved her toward the man, and the "bum" (who was actually Tim) got down on his knee and asked her to marry him. "I was in complete shock!" said Jenny. "Then I recognized my boyfriend and hit him on the shoulder, telling him to take those fake teeth out!"

Tim had obviously not gone hunting. Instead he'd spent the day disguising himself as a 50-year-old homeless man. Stage makeup, fake moustache and beard, fake teeth, glasses and a "homeless" costume made his transformation complete. "Tim is always full of surprises, and I should have known the proposal would be no different," said Jenny.

♥

Spike the Bulldog

Stephan and Melissa

It was the second half of the basketball game at Spokane's Gonzaga University when Melissa's name was called for a halfcourt-shot contest during the official time-out. Little did she know that it was her boyfriend, Stephan, behind the mascot's "Spike the Bulldog" mask.

As Melissa took her place on the basketball court, Stephan stood in front of her, removed his Bulldog hat, and knelt down on one knee with an open ring box. It took a moment for her to grasp the situation, but when the auditorium's screens began flashing "Melissa, please marry me — Stephan," she quickly threw down the basketball and said, "Yes!" The crowd, which included the two seniors' parents, went wild.

An added bonus: "Fox Sports filmed the whole event," said Stephan, "so now we can watch it over and over again."

The Kayak Proposal

Mark and Gina

Shortly after Mark and Gina began dating, Mark started what was to be the first of many homebuilt sea kayaks. Gina soon "persuaded" him to build a second one for her. The project began to drag on, and many believed that neither kayak would ever venture beyond Mark's apartment.

As these labors of love became an integral part of their dating years, Mark knew they had to be part of their engagement story as well. He was a bit apprehensive about the idea of proposing in a kayak, but he knew it would be a story for their grandchildren if he could pull it off.

Finally, the kayaks were ready to go. Mark loaded up his Jeep and the couple headed to the lake. After Mark received a tongue-lashing from a lifeguard for attempting to launch from a swimming area, forgot to adjust the foot braces in Gina's kayak, and accidentally hit her on the head with his paddle, the evening was off to a rocky start.

They paddled around for 30 minutes and then Mark, who could think of nothing but the intended proposal, said he thought they should call it a night. He let Gina paddle ahead and then intentionally rolled his kayak. She turned around and couldn't help laughing at him — completely drenched and clinging to his kayak — but backtracked to give him a hand. As she did, Mark held up a ring, securely attached to a flotation device. Bobbing up and down on one knee, Mark asked Gina to marry him and placed the ring on her finger, flotation device and all.

Best Buy Birthday

Jim and Shannon

*W*ith her boyfriend out of town and no big birthday plans, Shannon arrived at Best Buy expecting nothing. Suspecting nothing. She was there to help pick out a plasma television for her friend's husband. Nothing more, nothing less. But as Shannon and her friend began perusing televisions, Shannon's boyfriend, Jim, suddenly appeared on the screen in front of her. In fact, he was on all the TVs in the store. A two-minute prerecorded message showed Jim wishing Shannon a happy birthday and apologizing for being out of town on her special day.

But he wasn't out of town. And this wasn't just a birthday message. Jim was actually in the back of the store with Shannon's entire family. As Shannon watched and laughed at her missing boyfriend's thoughtful recording, the Jim on the TV went from birthday message to confessions of love and then a request for her to turn around so he could ask her a "very important question." And there stood Jim. Wearing a tuxedo and carrying roses, he dropped to one knee.

♥

The Bridge

Eric and Danielle

Danielle was finishing a double shift at work when Eric called and asked if she had enough energy to go out for dinner. She agreed, and he apologetically requested that she go a bit out of her way and meet him by "the bridge" — a little bridge over a creek that they often walked by, holding hands, and where they'd had their first date. Eric said he wanted to walk by the water with her for a bit, then grab a bite to eat. Danielle agreed, and left to meet him.

As she walked around the familiar bend of trees and saw the bridge, she was astounded. Christmas lights hung all over and under the bridge, their reflections dancing on the water like fireflies. A candlelight picnic dinner was set up, and a scrapbook was out. The couple ate, then Eric took the book out and they looked through it together. He had saved movie tickets from their first date and had other pieces of memorabilia worked in with baby pictures of her that he'd gotten from her mother.

After going through pages and pages of happy memories, he turned to the last page. A ring was tied with ribbon to the page, and there was a note saying, "I want to grow old with you. I want to spend every moment with you. Please marry me!"

Home Turf

Tim and Mo both loved baseball. They met during the Seattle Mariners' playoff run in 2000, and baseball had always played a big role in their relationship, especially because Tim worked as the assistant groundskeeper for the Mariners and spent a lot of time at Safeco Field. So he thought it only fitting to propose to Mo on home turf.

Tim picked a day in June when the Mariners were on the road and told Mo that he had to go in to work to mow a new pattern in the outfield grass. Later that afternoon, he called to say that he was having car trouble and asked her to pick him up. When she arrived, he invited her to come take a look at the new pattern in the grass. The couple took the elevator up to the 300-level and walked out behind home plate. As planned, they had the stadium to themselves. Looking over the railing, Mo had a little surprise waiting: "Mo, Will You Marry Me?" was written on the infield dirt. Then Tim got down on one knee and pulled out the ring.

Three months later, the couple got married at home plate.

In the News

Ryan and Karen

*R*yan and Karen met on stage while performing with their local community theater — just before rehearsing their kissing scene. He knew immediately that she was the one. And the kiss only confirmed the feeling.

Given Karen's penchant for the stage, he thought it appropriate to create a proposal moment that was symbolic of her love and flair for the dramatic. The couple lived in a small town a few hours south of Seattle, the kind of place where everyone knows who you are. And he wanted everyone to see what he had planned and what he had to say.

With the help of some creative photography, Ryan captured a moment when she was looking downward at something cooking on the stove with a somewhat perplexed expression. Then he had a picture taken of him kneeling and looking up. Using photo-editing software, Ryan manipulated the pictures so that it looked like he was on one knee on a tropical beach, gazing up into her eyes and asking her to marry him, while she was looking down at him. Then he purchased a quarter-page, full-color space in the local newspaper to run the message on Thanksgiving morning. Karen was an avid reader of the daily paper, so he was sure she'd find it.

That morning, a video camera was running as she turned the page — so the couple can relive the 59 times that Karen exclaimed "Oh my God" that morning.

Jailhouse Rock

Jamie and Amber

*J*amie had to take a business trip to San Francisco and invited his girlfriend, Amber, to go along. After he'd finished his work, the couple set out to visit the standard tourist traps: Ghirardelli Square, Farmers Market, SBC Park and, of course, Alcatraz.

After the 40-minute tour of Alcatraz, Jamie told Amber there was something he wanted to look at, and she followed him to the D block. He then led Amber into an open cell, where he put her hands into the pocket of his pullover sweatshirt and slipped an engagement ring onto her finger, asking, "Would you be my cellmate for a life sentence?"

No Pearl?

Kris and Kristin

Kristin had convinced herself that Valentine's Day was too perfect an occasion for a proposal — so perfect that it was highly unlikely her boyfriend would actually pick that date. So when Kris took her to dinner at the Crab Pot, where they'd had their first date, she was not suspicious. The staff unloaded a bowl of shellfish directly onto their tabletop, and armed with bibs and mallets, the couple began to eat. At the bottom of the pile, there was a single oyster. "How'd that get there?" Kristin thought.

Unbeknownst to her, Kris had sneaked the oyster in when she wasn't looking. In fact, he had earlier picked up the oyster at the market, cleaned it, and even lined it with velvet and attached a hinge.

Had she known this, Kristin would have acted a little differently. Instead, trying to be coy, she picked up the oyster and — rather than opening it to reveal its prize — played ventriloquist and made it say "I love you" to her boyfriend. He looked sick rather than amused, and Kristin was confused. She decided to go ahead and enjoy the lone oyster in the pile, and was shocked to open the shell and find not a pearl but "the most beautiful diamond engagement ring."

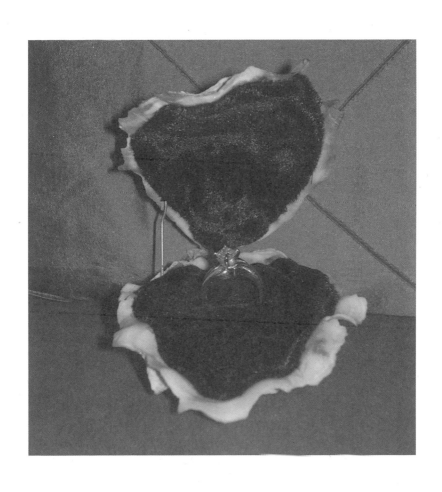

Impromptu Inspiration

Ed and Margaret

*E*d knew he would propose that day at the beach. The question was in the details. As they walked along hand in hand, the couple came across a historic church. Both being Catholic, they went in to pray. And Ed made sure to ask for divine guidance.

The couple then strolled along the beach, talking about the things that were special to them. They came across some old wooden steps and sat down to watch the sun set. Ed's heart raced. He knew this was the time. This was the spot. And he got down on one knee with words of love and adoration.

He found a wildflower nearby and gave it to Margaret, saying, "May this flower represent the beauty that I have found in you, and tell you how special you are in my life." He also found a seashell, gave it to her and continued, "May this shell represent to you how strong our relationship is, and yet how fragile it can be. And like the seashell, it has to be taken care of so it can endure many years and many obstacles in front of it."

Lastly, Ed found a matchbook with two matches inside. He gave it to his intended and said, "May these matches let you know that there is always a light at the end of the tunnel, and that no matter what life has in store for us, we can always see the light at the end together. So with these things, would you also take this ring and marry me?" And Margaret responded with happy tears and a joyful "Yes, I will."

Mid-Court Surprise

Jasen and Tanya

After nine months of dating, Tanya conspired with her big brother Eddie to beat Jasen to the proposal punch. Courtside tickets in hand, Eddie invited Sonics mega-fan Jasen to join him at a game. They arrived early to watch warm-ups and were asked if one of them would like to participate in the Sonics' first-quarter entertainment. Tanya's brother quickly deferred to his guest. The staff explained that Jasen would be playing the "hot or cold" game, where he would wear a blindfold and try to find the team's mascot, Squatch, in less than a minute. The crowd would cheer or boo according to whether he was headed in the right direction. If he found Squatch, he was told, he would win an autographed team jersey.

Out on the court, the blindfold went on and the crowd went crazy. Jasen thought they were rooting for him to win. He didn't know that the screen above read: "Please, help Jasen find his future wife, we hope." With the help of the crowd, the blindfolded Jasen located the mascot. Squatch pulled off Jasen's blindfold and turned him around — and there stood his girlfriend. He started to give Tanya a hug, but she put up her hand, dropped to her knees, pulled out a ring box and asked him to marry her. Jasen fell to his knees, grabbed Tanya's face and kissed her.

As the shock wore off, they stood up and Tanya pointed to the stands, where 40 of their friends and family stood in the crowd cheering, each holding a letter to form the message "I love Jasen. Will you marry me?"

Point of View

Shae and Meg

$\mathcal{T}$he weather wasn't cooperating with their desert camping trip, and Shae, Meg and their friend Julie had different ideas about what could and couldn't be done in the storm. As they pulled into Arches National Park in Utah, Meg suggested setting up camp in lieu of hiking. But Julie and Shae protested, insisting that they go on at least one hike before heading for the campsite. Meg agreed, but not happily. The group decided on a hike that would take them over slick desert rock to the base of Shae's favorite formation in the park, Delicate Arch.

Midway into the climb, Shae said he was feeling ill and asked to slow down. Julie insisted on continuing and quickly disappeared. Shae and Meg proceeded slowly up the trail. Just before the last section, as they hiked along a sheer rock ledge, the thunderstorm caught up with them. Stranded on the exposed ledge, Shae and Meg pulled their sweatshirts over their heads and huddled together while rain, hail, thunder and lightning surrounded them. Then, as quickly as it had come on, the storm subsided.

The couple rounded the final bend and saw Julie excitedly pointing at the arch, which was still out of sight. Just before they reached the view point, Shae asked Meg to stop and close her eyes, so that he could get her "in the perfect position to see the arch." She gave in, inching along and trusting that Shae wouldn't let her slip. Finally, he instructed her to open her eyes. She was startled to see her view of Delicate Arch blocked by Shae's hand, which was holding a ring.

Sinatra and the Space Needle

Jose and Stephanie

Stephanie arrived dressed to the nines at the Space Needle with no suspicions. Jose had told her they were there for a company dinner to celebrate a project. As they approached the Seattle icon, Jose called a co-worker to ask him to save them seats, the cue for Jose's pre-orchestrated plan to commence.

Upon their arrival, the receptionist led Stephanie and Jose into an elevator, where a group of people immediately — and intentionally — followed, making the couple stand toward the back of the glass elevator and blocking their view. The group quickly dispersed when they reached the restaurant level.

After excusing himself briefly to "use the restroom," Jose suggested that they go check out the view before dinner. So, back in the elevator they went. When the doors opened on the observation deck, Frank Sinatra's "The Way You Look Tonight" just "happened" to be playing. "Hey, that's our song!" exclaimed Stephanie. "Yeah, that's pretty cool," said Jose nonchalantly. "Let's go look at the skyline."

While they were enjoying the view, Jose looked toward the base of the Needle and, appearing confused, said, "What is that down there?" Stephanie leaned over and saw an enormous sign illuminated by a dozen floodlights that read: "Will You Marry Me, Stephanie?" She turned around in shock to find Jose down on one knee and the Space Needle's photographers waiting to capture the moment.

Glass Goblet

Tim and Sara

When it came time to propose, Tim turned to his art for romantic inspiration. He was a glassblower who employed the "lampworking" method, using rods of hard glass that became molten when heated in the flame of a torch. The method allowed for a more detailed product, sometimes incorporating small designs or text.

For their third anniversary, the couple decided to escape from the city and rent a small cabin in the mountains. They made a few stops before hitting the road, including one at Tim's glass studio. Sara thought nothing of it and waited in the car.

When they arrived at the cabin, both were thrilled. From the already-lit fire in the fireplace to the wonderful bed and luxurious sheets in the lofted bedroom, it was "incredibly cute and romantic," Sara recalled. They soon settled in, and Tim went to open a bottle of their favorite wine. Sara came into the kitchen and found him standing over two gorgeous goblets he had hand-blown for her. She was so impressed and surprised that she didn't notice how nervous he was.

The couple sat on the floor in front of the fire, talking and drinking their wine. At one point, Tim exclaimed that Sara was taking too long to drink hers. So she "stopped talking so much and started really taking sips." When she had about three sips left, she noticed something in the glass. Swigging the last few sips, Sara discovered that at the bottom of the cup, Tim had written in the glass, with glass, "Marry Me."

Prescription: Marriage

Brian and Jennifer

*I*t was time, Brian decided. He had recently graduated from pharmacy school, and Jennifer was in her final year. So a few days before Thanksgiving, he told Jennifer he wanted to take her to dinner before the holiday chaos began. He picked her up at the end of a long day of school and work, and they headed to her favorite restaurant, where Brian planned to propose. But some friends were seated nearby and, not wanting to make a huge show out of his proposal, Brian decided to wait.

After dinner, the couple took a stroll around downtown Seattle. Brian's "Plan B" was to propose in the light of the nearby plaza's towering Christmas tree. The tree was there, but it apparently would remain dark until after Thanksgiving.

The couple returned to Jennifer's apartment. A tired Jennifer changed into pajamas as Brian paced in the living room. He knew it was his last chance. He reached into his jacket, pulled out a labeled prescription vial, and told Jennifer she had to see it, as the doctor had done something "really funny." She took the vial, and soon the tiredness vanished and a smile spread across her face.

On the label was Jennifer's name with the following instructions: "Place this ring on your finger and take Brian to be your husband." Inside the vial was her engagement ring, gently resting on a bed of cotton.

Treasure Hunt

Michael and Tara

One sunny spring morning, Michael took Tara down to their favorite beach to walk along the shore, where they "discovered" a cobalt blue bottle partially buried in the sand. Tara removed the cork and found a piece of parchment paper inside that described a hidden treasure and sent them on a journey to find it. The note said they would find something at the base of Snoqualmie Falls, under an arrowhead-shaped rock. Tara smiled suspiciously at Michael, and off they went. As they drove, they listened to their usual '50s station, and every song seemed to be one of their favorites. (Michael had secretly set up a radio transmitter in the trunk with a tape of their favorite songs.)

When they arrived at the falls, they hiked to the base. The couple spotted the arrowhead-shaped rock and climbed down to it. Underneath was a small wooden box. Inside was a brass key on a blue string necklace and a map. The map guided them onto secluded trails and up a hidden path that led to a moss-covered log on a quiet hillside. Tara sat down and waited patiently while Michael searched around under the moss. He *finally* found what he was looking for, a small box shaped like a treasure chest. Tara unlocked it to find her great-grandmother's engagement ring inside.

Years later, the arrowhead rock rests in the couple's garden; the blue bottle with the note inside, the little treasure chest and the brass key sit on their bedroom dresser. "They remind me that making special memories during the journey through life is indeed the treasure itself," said Michael.

Underwater Treasure

Steven and Chris

*S*teven and Chris's relationship grew steadily over months of scuba diving togéther. So, ready to propose, Steven knew he'd have to take her breath away — underwater. He reserved spaces on a dive-boat charter and told Chris that several friends would be joining them. Utilizing some items left over from an underwater pirate movie they had filmed with friends, Steven weighted a little black velvet box with lead, placed a costume ring inside (he wasn't about to gamble on losing the real thing), put the box in a treasure chest and securely fastened the chest.

When the group reached the islands, their friends jumped into the water first and took some glow sticks and the treasure chest to an underwater shelf that circumvented one small island at about 25 feet below the surface. They set up a trail of lights, positioned the treasure chest at the end, and lay in wait with the camera rolling. Steven and Chris then entered the water.

Under normal circumstances, the couple would descend to the deepest spot, then proceed back up the wall, exploring along the way. But partway down, Steven motioned for Chris to come back up to where he was. She followed him and soon noticed the glow sticks placed along the ledge. Then she discovered the treasure chest, surrounded by even more glow sticks. Carefully opening it, she peered in and found a black box. "My heart was his," said Chris. The captain of the boat then proceeded to officially rename that specific spot on Willows Island "Proposal Point."

Note Afloat

Dustin and Stefanie

Dustin and Stefanie were celebrating their 10-month anniversary at the restaurant where they'd had their first date. By coincidence, or so thought Stefanie, they were even seated at the exact same table.

After dinner, Dustin suggested that they take a walk around nearby Green Lake. While they were sitting at the edge of the lake, enjoying the view, Dustin pointed out a bottle floating in the water. Curious, Stefanie picked it up and realized it was a corked bottle with a message inside. She opened the bottle and found a romantic poem about their love. The first letter of each sentence, read downward, spelled out "MARRY ME."

Easter Egg Hunt

Aaron and Michelle

On Easter eve, Aaron waited for Michelle to go to sleep, then put together a special Easter basket for her and hid plastic eggs all over the house in preparation for "the hunt." Some of the eggs glowed in the dark. Some had suction cups. Some hung from string. He put them in the garage, the refrigerator and the microwave, suctioned one to the computer monitor and one to the bathroom mirror, and even put one in a bird feeder on their deck.

The first clue egg was placed right beside her basket, which took Michelle a while to find because she was having so much fun with everything else in the basket. But once she'd found it, she was off and running. The last egg held the following clue: "Roses are red; violets are blue; come to your bedroom and I will show how much I love you."

Michelle entered the darkened room in search of her final clue and could just barely make out the little table Aaron had prepared with white linen, champagne flutes and their favorite sparkling wine. Then Aaron came out of the dark, got down on one knee, and held up a specially designed ring box with a light inside that illuminated the ring as he asked Michelle to be his wife.

A Fortune for Him

Philip and Lisa

Lisa knew that Philip wanted to propose. And she wanted him to. But after Philip had to replace his car's engine, she didn't think he'd have money for a ring anytime soon. Lisa knew that he wouldn't propose without one, so she secretly had a ring made with stones from a family piece — and had a ring made for him as well.

Finally, it was their anniversary, and the ring set was finished. So Lisa invited Philip out for sushi, their favorite meal. For dessert, she gave him a box of fortune cookies she had made herself. The cookies were numbered, and the enclosed fortunes started out fun and got progressively more serious. Through her series of fortunes, Lisa told him she couldn't be with him every day (work had caused them to move three hours apart) and that he was the person she wanted to spend her life with.

Fortune cookie number seven included his ring, which he figured was an anniversary present. The next fortune read, "Marry me." Shocked to say the least, he did say yes. In the last cookie was her ring. "He was so thankful because he so desperately wanted to propose but couldn't afford the ring he wanted," Lisa said. He still plans to buy her a ring, but while they wait for that day, they're getting married.

The Movie Cameo

Kurt and Jaimie

On their first date, they saw the movie *Singles*, based on the dating scene during Seattle's grunge era. Ironically, neither was single after that. And after six months, Kurt knew that Jaimie was the woman for him and suggested that they watch their first-date movie again, which had just been released to home video. After all, he suggested, what better way to celebrate?

What Jaimie didn't know was that Kurt had copied the movie to another VHS tape and spliced himself into the film as if he were a character in the movie. (The movie has numerous "interviews" with the different cast members talking about their experiences dating in Seattle, so Kurt just added his own.)

About 30 minutes into the movie, Kurt's face popped up on the screen. In real life, he was sweating. His lines? "Dating in Seattle has been great, but when you know that you have met the right woman, you ask her to marry you! Jaimie, will you marry me?"

After his "cameo," Jaimie turned to him in disbelief. Kurt then held up the ring he had hidden in the couch and asked her to marry him. She said yes, and they still have the tape to prove it. Evidence, Kurt says, of his younger and skinnier days.

The Wishing Chair

Jeffrey and Christine

"Remember the night of our first dance," read the card attached to the rose that Christine found on her nightstand. When she quizzed Jeffrey about it, he shrugged. "Must be a rose gnome running around." Then he casually suggested going out for breakfast. The couple split a farmer's omelet, and with the check came another rose. "Wow," Jeffrey said. "What great service." Then he recommended going to the movies. At the theater, the usher ripped and returned their ticket stubs — with another rose. "Well," Jeffrey said, "we must've been the millionth customer or something." It was like that all day. Walking around a nearby lake, they discovered a rose every 10 minutes. A rose was on their table when they sat down to dinner, and another came with their check.

As they strolled along a city street, a woman at a door suddenly said, "Two for the observation deck?" They followed her in and rode to the 35th floor, where they stepped out into a beautifully ornate room at the top of a downtown office building. There sat the "Wishing Chair," surrounded by four dozen roses. The legend of this elaborately carved blackwood chair was that any wishful unmarried woman who sits in it will be married the next year. On the seat lay the final rose with the final card. Jeffrey picked up the rose, handed it to Christine, and asked her to have a seat as he brought out the ring that had been burning a hole in his pocket all day. The final card read: "Remember that day when I proposed to you."

Geocaching Adventure

Josh and Elizabeth

Elizabeth and Josh had been planning to go geocaching for quite some time. Geocaching involves using a handheld GPS unit to locate a treasure, or cache, hidden by participants who then post the latitude and longitude coordinates online for other participants to find. Elizabeth was eager to finally get to do it.

The couple piled into Josh's Jeep with two friends and headed off in search of hidden treasure. Little did Elizabeth know that the stack of printed directions included an impostor. To ensure that their final destination was for Elizabeth's eyes only, Josh had worked with the geocaching website's owners to fake an official cache location.

Their friend Reina easily found the first real cache, an old ammunition box filled with an assortment of key chains. Josh found the next one, and the group decided to try for one more, called "Twin Falls." With a little help from her friends, Elizabeth found the spot beside the river where the cache should be. After some extra guidance from Josh, she discovered the box and opened it.

"I saw a stack of letters — 50 or more — from all my family and friends," Elizabeth said. The top letter was from her dad. Confused, she began to read: "Congratulations on your wedding announcement to Josh."

Elizabeth looked at Josh, who took her hands in his and dropped to one knee. Covering the ring box with one hand, he told her that she couldn't see her treasure until she located an answer. She said yes, and their day of adventure became their most memorable day ever.

Sleigh Ride for Two

Chris and Tara

The tree-lighting festival at Leavenworth was an annual tradition for Chris and Tara. Surrounded by snow-covered peaks and evergreens, the Bavarian-themed mountain town is postcard perfect. But something was a little different this particular year, Tara said. Chris was letting her have or do whatever she wished — "I felt like a princess," she said.

On the second day of the trip, however, Chris announced that they were going on a sleigh ride. This was generally a group affair, but Chris insisted on paying extra to make it a sleigh for two. "It was perfect seeing the snow across the mountains in the background as we cuddled under a blanket," Tara remembered.

When they reached the Icicle River, where the flowing water causes many icicles to form — a spectacular sight — Chris asked the sleigh driver to stop. Then he got down on one knee and told Tara that she was the woman he wanted to spend the rest of his life with.

"I could have never imagined a more romantic proposal," said Tara. "The sleigh driver told us that every year when he comes upon the river, he will tell about our proposal."

A Theatrical Proposal

Michael and Wendy

$\mathcal{M}$ichael and Wendy both loved the stage, so when he invited her to join him for a performance at a favorite childhood outdoor theater, Wendy was more than happy to oblige. The musical was *Oliver*, and Wendy was thoroughly enjoying herself. Everything seemed normal. Before intermission, actors dressed as London policemen said they had a demonstration and asked for volunteers. Michael volunteered himself and Wendy, and they were called on to demonstrate a "pickpocket," as seen in the first half of the musical, using the *Oliver* handkerchiefs that would be on sale during intermission. Wendy's only thought was "Aha! They want to sell their goods!"

As instructed, Wendy picked Michael's handkerchief out of his pocket. Then one of the "policemen" announced that he had witnessed a crime of pickpocketing, that this was a serious offense, and that Michael would read Wendy her rights from a formal citation. Wendy was confused. That is, until Michael turned around with a huge sign that read: "Wendy, will you marry me?"

♥

J. P. Patches Pal

Gene and Lisa

$\mathcal{L}$isa was a longtime fan of J. P. Patches, a well-known clown to many who grew up in the Northwest. A "Patches Pal" from way back, she had submitted countless photos to his television show and even appeared on the show with her Brownie troop. Gene had grown up on the East Coast and knew nothing about J. P. Patches.

One evening, Gene surprised Lisa by taking her to a fancy downtown Seattle restaurant for dinner. They had barely started their meal when Gene set aside his napkin, got down on one knee, took Lisa's hand in his and asked her to be his wife. She immediately accepted. Then Gene presented Lisa with a very sweet, square, plastic neon clown ring. He told her he couldn't yet afford much, and that he hoped she understood.

As the couple hugged, J. P. Patches appeared at their table — the real Julius Pierpont Patches. The beloved clown said he had heard that one of his Patches Pals had just gotten engaged. He took one look at Lisa's ring and told Gene that it just wouldn't do. After fishing around in his baggy clown pants, J. P. Patches presented Lisa with a small gift-wrapped box. "Inside was the most beautiful diamond ring I'd ever seen," she remembered.

Later, Lisa wanted to invite her favorite clown to the wedding, but she couldn't find his address. Her soon-to-be husband reassured her, saying that special things happened for loyal Patches Pals. Sure enough, Lisa spotted J. P. Patches among her reception guests. "We talked and laughed, and he warmed the hearts of many guests," Lisa recalled. And when she saw the clown saying his farewells, "I tapped him on that old familiar patchwork shoulder and asked him for the last dance."

Over the Rooftops

*S*arah didn't suspect a thing when her boyfriend of two years casually invited her to the Space Needle one afternoon. She wasn't really a tourist-spot person, but Mike convinced her that it would be something different. When they got to the top of the Emerald City icon, Sarah was unimpressed. Mike walked over to the binoculars, put a quarter in and encouraged her to take a look around. While she was occupied, he reached into his pocket and hit speed-dial. On the other end of the call, his friend Rick picked up the phone and then hung up. Mike's plan had been set in motion.

Sarah was still aimlessly scanning Puget Sound and the surrounding hills when a strobe light suddenly lit up on one of the rooftops. Mike pointed it out, and she immediately homed in on the signal, which was illuminating a huge white sheet made of sewn-together bedspreads that hung over the apartment building below. It read: "Sarah, will you marry me!!"

Bewildered, Sarah turned around to see Mike on his knees with a ring, asking, "So, whaddya think?"

Sarah responded, "Of course! I'll marry any man that I'd follow to a touristy place . . . and one that would be crazy enough to cover a house with my name."

A Starry Night

George and Rebekah

George and Rebekah were stargazers. They enjoyed long walks in the dark, looking at the constellations, and they even had their names added to the gold disk on the Mars probe before it launched.

One day he took Rebekah to the planetarium at the Pacific Science Center, where the curator made a personal presentation for George, Rebekah, her two children, and a close friend. The presentation just "happened" to focus on things that the couple routinely looked at in the sky. At the end, the curator said she thought George had a question. As the music from *Sleepless in Seattle* played in the background and the planetarium's stars began to glow brighter, George got down on one knee. Rebekah, of course, said yes. And the stars have forever shone brighter for the two of them.

Propose like a
Rock Star

Tino and Jacki

$\mathcal{T}$hey were already married, had two kids, and had survived the ups and downs of military life. Tino had long ago asked Jacki's parents for her hand in marriage, but he'd never proposed in the memorable way that he thought his beloved deserved. So when he heard about the "Propose like a Rock Star" opportunity on Seattle's radio station KISS 106.1, he knew he had to try.

And as it happened, Tino won the prize. He told Jacki he'd won some concert tickets, but the rest she never suspected. As the couple — and their two children — waited in Key Arena for the concert to start, Jacki was blissfully unaware of what was to come when deejay Kristen "The Island Girl" came on stage and introduced "The Proposer." The mystery delivery man from E.E. Robbins, Seattle's Engagement Ring Store and one of the contest's co-sponsors, was dressed in black from head to toe and carried a steel briefcase handcuffed to his wrist containing the contest's prize, a beautiful wedding ring.

The Proposer made his way through the darkened arena with a spotlight tracing his steps. As the tall, handsome man in black approached, Jacki was convinced that he was about to propose to the girl sitting next to her. Then Kristen announced, "Congratulations to Tino and Jacki!" Jacki gasped. They'd been married for a dozen years, but Tino was a nervous young man once again. He quickly gathered his wits, got down on bended knee and held out the open ring box, saying, "Jacki, will you continue to be the love of my life and do me the honor of being my wife?" There was no hesitation in her reply: "Yes." It was the best prize Tino could imagine. "I wanted to show her that I do love her a lot," he said. And why not let her know in front of 10,000 screaming concertgoers?

What a Crab!

Adam and Rachael

*R*achael thought it was going to be just another sunny summer afternoon. They had waited for months for crabbing season to open, and she was looking forward to taking the boat out. Adam couldn't wait either, but he had more than crabbing in mind. He had gone out earlier to set up the crab pots, and had not only intentionally set them in front of a beach that had meaning for them both, but also included a few "extras" in one of the traps.

Later in the day, with Rachael by his side, Adam was ready to put his plan into action. When it came time to pull up the second pot, he said that his back was hurting and asked Rachael to pull it up. Without thinking much of it, she began to haul in the 100 feet of rope. As the pot came closer and closer to the surface, she could see that there was one crab in the center. Next, she noticed that this crab was holding a red paper heart — not your usual crabbing sight. Then she read the paper: "Rachael, will you marry me?"

Adam pulled a ring out of his pocket and proposed right there on the boat. "I must say," said Rachael, "that was the best crab pot I ever pulled up."

Umbrella at the Falls

Steve and Ilana

*I*t was the day after Valentine's Day, and both Steve and Ilana had some time off from school. That afternoon, the couple headed out to Snoqualmie Falls for a drizzly hike. Just as they pulled into the parking lot, the rain subsided. When they reached the overlook at the top of the falls, Ilana noticed that Steve had brought an umbrella. "What did you bring that for?" Real Seattleites don't use umbrellas. He muttered some lame response, and off they trudged down the muddy path.

When they got to the next overlook, Ilana saw something unusual on the boulders below. "Let's get closer," Steve suggested. As they neared the tumbling falls, Ilana saw that the dots of red she had seen from above were the tops of roses in shot glasses. The roses and a dusting of gold glitter marked a shimmering pathway toward the falls. Ilana figured the display must be left over from Valentine's Day. Then she saw her name spelled out in silver glitter on a large boulder, with a huge red heart sparkling below it.

"Look at the falls," said Steve, as he hugged her from behind. "Choose a point where the water is falling and don't take your eyes off that spot." After about half a minute, he told her to look at the sheer rock wall next to the falls. Ilana gasped as the rocks appeared to move, sway and grow. Then Steve said, "Now I hope you're dizzy enough to say yes" and opened the umbrella. Hanging from fishing wire were glittery letters that read: "MARRY ME."

Dr. Seuss Style

Mike and Diane

Diane and Mike had dated for just over two years and had never discussed marriage when he surprised her with "the question" while they soaked in a hot tub during a vacation in Whistler, B.C. It started playfully. Lightheartedly even. She had no reason to suspect anything. Mike led in with a familiar-sounding rhyme:

> Would you, could you, here or there?
> Would you, could you, anywhere?

Diane responded:

> Would you, could you, on the lawn?
> Would you, could you, from dusk 'til dawn?

The rhymes went back and forth as the pair laughed at their rewriting of *Green Eggs and Ham.* After about 10 minutes and many verses, it was Mike's turn again. He pulled out a ring from beneath his towel, took Diane's hand and asked:

> Would you, could you, all my life?
> Marry me and be my wife?

After about half an hour, Diane regained her composure long enough to ask if she had said yes yet. "I shook my head," Mike said. "And it's been an incredible 18 years together since she responded at that moment with an excited 'Yes!' "

By Personal Invitation

James and Joon

*O*ne day, an e-mail arrived in Joon's inbox with the subject line "EMP Invitation — Private Music Video Screening." The message said that selected Experience Music Project members were invited to bring a guest and screen a new artist's upcoming album and music video. Drinks and appetizers were complimentary, of course. Joon called James instantly, thank goodness.

Two weeks later, the couple arrived at EMP, where they were greeted by staff and given admission bracelets and informational materials about the event. They were then taken to the private screening room, which was decorated with blue lighting, a red velvet couch, a few dozen roses and several candles. A large flat-panel screen hung in the middle of the room.

The couple sat down, and then the lights dimmed and the screen flickered on: "Enter the Proposal." Rather than a music video, they heard their favorite song, and then a personal video that James had made for Joon began to play. The video detailed how they met, dated and fell in love. At the end, he got down on one knee. And James has confirmed that a happy ending ensued.

♥

Underwater Cheese

Mark and Chantelle

A few weeks before Mark and Chantelle's vacation to Australia for some scuba diving, he purchased a special slate and pencil set to write on underwater. She gave him grief about it, saying it was "cheesy" and that they'd never use it. He bought it anyway.

In Australia, the couple went on a dive by themselves on a cool shipwreck. After checking out the sights, they had to hover underwater to decompress before surfacing. Chantelle held on to Mark as he used his "cheesy" slate and pencil to write "Chantelle, Will You Marry Me?" When he turned it around for her to read, she just froze, stunned. Then the words finally sank in, and she nodded happily as they took their regulators out of their mouths for a celebration kiss — all underwater.

Ring or Remodel

Billy and Courtney

$\mathcal{B}$illy had always told Courtney that he would buy her an engagement ring after they purchased a house. But when the time came, he wanted it to be a bit more "spontaneous," so he told her that she might have to wait, that it was either the ring or the kitchen cabinets. She didn't know that this was part of Billy's plan, or that the day they closed on their house, he went out and personally designed and ordered a custom engagement ring.

While waiting for the ring, Billy made good use of his time. He rented a seaplane and enlisted family help — asking his parents to stock an island cabin with champagne, flowers and candles, arranging for his mother and a friend to take photos of the proposal, and even orchestrating a post-proposal celebration with both of their families.

When the day arrived, Billy surprised Courtney with a romantic dinner followed by a seaplane ride to their weekend getaway. Admittedly, when he grabbed a previously packed bag out of the trunk and asked Courtney if she was coming, "she had to know," said Billy. But her occasional tears of joy and anticipation hardly ruined the surprises that awaited her.

The plane landed in front of the island cabin, and the couple walked along the beach until Billy dropped the bags, reached for the ring and declared his undying love for Courtney. With a big yes and a long kiss, the deal was sealed. The next morning, the two headed back to the beach to carve their initials, the date and the depiction of a ring into a log at the exact spot of their proposal.

Funny Papers

Joe and Patti

"What's going on?" asked Patti when her boyfriend, Joe, arrived home early with a bouquet of a dozen roses.

"I got one of my comic strips published," Joe responded.

Patti was excited for him, especially since she'd had no idea that he'd been trying to do that. Then she read it.

In the first frame, it showed Melvin (Joe's character) quoting a poem that Mr. Cartoonist (Joe) had written to his girlfriend. The poem read:

> Pop bottles have caps,
> Pickle jars have lids,
> Patti, please marry me
> and have my kids.

The last frame showed butterflies flitting around. Melvin asked what was with all the butterflies. Mr. Cartoonist replied, "Sorry, Melvin — those are mine."

Patti was reading this as Joe bent down on his knees with the engagement ring. "She was speechless," Joe remembered, "but here we are married nine years later, with me still drawing cartoons for her."

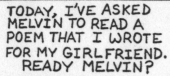

The Perfect Topping

Brian and Kerri

*B*rian was a "lifelong bachelor" when he and Kerri began dating. Never been married. No kids. And he lived very simply. His favorite food? Pizza. So when Kerri decided it was time to ask her boyfriend to marry her, she wanted to make it personal.

"Our favorite time together was watching movies, eating pizza and hanging out on the couch," Kerri said. "I wanted to catch him totally off-guard, when he would never expect it." So she called in a very special pizza order for delivery, picked up movies and headed home.

It was a "typical" Friday night. Nothing out of the ordinary. Kerri was setting up the movie when the pizza got there. Brian brought it down, box and all, with plates and drinks. Since Brian always served her, Kerri knew he would be the first to see the pizza. And there, on the pepperoni pizza, spelled out ever so carefully in black olives, was "Will You Marry Me?" — a perfectly prepared pizza proposal!

By the Light
of the Harvest Moon

Bob and Koko

There would be a full harvest moon. Vega was expected to make an appearance directly overhead. And Venus would be in view to the west. The forecast was good as they drove up the dusty road to the trailhead on Mount Townsend, in the northern Olympic Mountains.

The trail was steep, especially with a full backpack, but they reached camp and pitched their tent next to a little lake in the woods. Bob quickly made dinner and suggested a hike. He packed his "secret stash," and he and Koko reached the mountain's top before sunset. It was an impressive view. The couple settled in a patch of high dry grass behind a bank of black volcanic rocks and watched the sun set.

After sunset, Koko suspected that a proposal might be imminent. It started to get cold, and Bob pulled out a sleeping bag. The few other hikers left, and Koko didn't understand why they were still there, but Bob persuaded her to stay. It grew darker, and finally a huge orange moon rose. The two of them then watched the new celestial spectacle. Koko settled into her sleeping bag, and Bob pulled out headphones and played a recording of Neil Young's "Harvest Moon." And then — under this harvest moon — he proposed.

Marshall's Marriage Proposal

Marshall and Emily

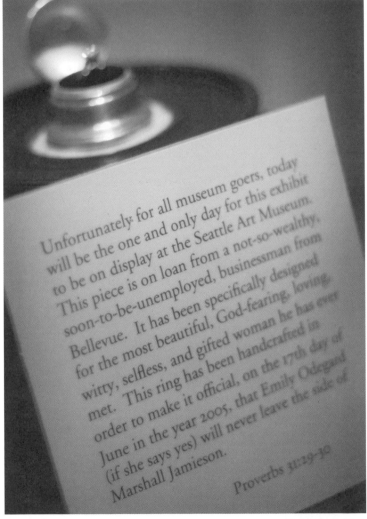

Unfortunately for all museum goers, today will be the one and only day for this exhibit to be on display at the Seattle Art Museum. This piece is on loan from a not-so-wealthy, soon-to-be-unemployed, businessman from Bellevue. It has been specifically designed for the most beautiful, God-fearing, loving, witty, selfless, and gifted woman he has ever met. This ring has been handcrafted in order to make it official, on the 17th day of June in the year 2005, that Emily Odegard (if she says yes) will never leave the side of Marshall Jamieson.

Proverbs 31:29-30

Photo: Bryan Myss

*M*arshall was about to take off on a five-week trip, and he couldn't bear to say farewell to Emily without assuring her of his return. So he suggested a *Ferris Bueller's Day Off* scenario for the Friday before his departure.

The adventure began with a picturesque hike, a scrumptious lunch and a relaxing walk along the pier. The next stop: the Seattle Art Museum. And that day, there was a special exhibit. After they had wandered around for a while, Marshall directed Emily's attention to a display in the main exhibit room. Behind the glass, perched on a beautifully carved Asian wood stand, sat a bell-shaped silver jewelry box, in which nested an exquisite solitaire diamond ring. "How beautiful," she exclaimed, and began to read the plaque:

> Unfortunately for all museum-goers, today will be the one and only day for this exhibit to be on display at the Seattle Art Museum. This piece is on loan from a not-so-wealthy, soon-to-be-unemployed businessman from Bellevue. It has been specifically designed for the most beautiful, God-fearing, loving, witty, selfless and gifted woman he has ever met. This ring has been handcrafted in order to make it official, on the 17th day of June in the year 2005, that Emily (if she says yes) will never leave the side of Marshall. Proverbs 31:29-30

Emily's jaw dropped as she whispered to Marshall, "Are you kidding me?" He wasn't kidding, and he lifted the glass case off the display and knelt before Emily with ring in hand.

Red Baron

Dubs and Rebecca

*T*heir eyes met across a sea of singles during a concert at Seattle's Experience Music Project, and the connection was immediate. Their one-year anniversary could easily have been the day that he proposed. Instead, the lovebirds spent their anniversary frolicking on the Oregon coast, taking pictures that would soon become their engagement photos.

Dubs soon suggested a weekend trip to the San Juans, including a scenic flight over the islands. Rebecca was no fan of small, precarious airplanes, but she agreed to go. So, not even two weeks after their anniversary, the pair boarded a small four-seat Beaver airplane. Dubs was calm, cool, collected and very happy. Rebecca was nervous. But as the plane lifted and the scenery unfolded before them, she was easily distracted by the sunset hues above and the deep blue sea dotted with green islands below (and a special guy sitting next to her).

In the distance, an open-cockpit "Red Baron" biplane flew gracefully. The pilot soared in for a closer view and soon got a little too close for Rebecca's comfort. "Do you know those guys?" she asked nervously. When she looked again at the pretty little plane, she saw that it carried two pilots dressed in vintage leather helmets, billowing white scarves — and a sign that read: "Marry Dubs?"

Her reply was a resolute "Yes!" And out popped the ring that held his grandmother's and great-grandmother's diamonds. The rest, as they say, is history.

The Marry-Me Tree

Jon and Laurie

It was a lovely October evening, and Laurie
had just gotten home from work when Jon told her to
go look in the backyard. She noticed some charming
autumn crocuses growing off the deck. "Oh, they're
beautiful," she replied. But that wasn't what Jon was
talking about. "No, look farther back into the yard."
She didn't see anything.

Suddenly, a floodlight illuminated the backyard. Laurie
walked up the steps from the deck to an area of fruit
trees. Something was strung between them. Jon — who
Laurie describes as "an artist and quite creative with
found objects" — had crafted the words "MARRY ME"
out of cut branches and wood screws. The dot on the
exclamation mark was a ring box.

Bicycle Built for Two

Ken and Heather

_K_en had the ring. He just needed a plan. And his prayers were answered when some friends gave him a classic tandem bike. He immediately went to work fixing up the bike, having told Heather that he was helping some friends build a retaining wall and dock at their home. Ken polished rust out of fenders, touched up the paint, worked on the gears. He had a metalsmith make brackets for wicker baskets he had found to use as saddlebags. He even found a classic chrome horn with a squeeze bulb.

Early one Saturday, with a ring in his pocket and a plan in his head, Ken secured the finished tandem to the top of his car and drove home. He expected Heather to still be asleep. But she was up reading. So he sat down next to her, reached into his pocket, pulled out a ring box — in which he'd placed the key to the tandem's lock with a key chain that said "the key to my heart" — and asked Heather to marry him. "What is this?" she asked. "The key to my heart," he responded. "No, really, what is this?" she persisted. Then Ken led her outside. "I got an engagement bicycle," she said.

Heather unlocked the bike, and the couple rode together to the University of Puget Sound campus and parked next to the fountain, where Ken started to unload a picnic breakfast. He told her what he'd really been up to, and she continued to say things like: "I can't believe I got an engagement bicycle." Then Ken reached into the bottom of one of the saddlebags and pulled out the second ring box. Smiling, he asked, "Is this a little better?"

Magic Fountain

Michael and Lisa

They were in the middle of a dreamlike European trip through the likes of London, Paris and Florence when Michael put his plan into action. He and Lisa were walking across the heart of Rome, the Eternal City, when they came upon the magical Trevi Fountain. Even after a year of planning, he said, he still wasn't prepared for the hundreds of people that filled the square as they gazed at the magnificent fountain.

They walked down to the front of the fountain, where Michael turned on his video camera as usual and gave Lisa the "silver dollar" he had prepared for her, which included a special message engraved on the back. He asked Lisa if she was ready to throw her coin into the fountain. "Yes!" she said eagerly. Michael told her to turn her coin around first. She immediately noticed the tiny message inscribed at the bottom. It read: "Lisa, will you marry me? Love Mikey."

Michael bent down on his knee and whispered that there was a saying that when one throws a coin into the Trevi Fountain, it means you will come back there again someday, and that he hoped they would return to Rome as husband and wife. With that, Lisa happily tossed the coin into the fountain.

Sleight of Hand

Kerry and Dana

Kerry convinced Dana that they needed to stop by his place after dinner one evening. Inside the dark apartment, she flipped the switch and was dazzled by hundreds of white Christmas lights that Kerry had draped along every wall and across the ceiling of his living room. Every table and shelf was covered with rose petals, and four dozen roses were arranged in vases around the room.

Dana knew that Kerry didn't have much money, and she had mentioned that if he ever proposed, he didn't have to give her the "ring of her dreams." So, after leading her to the couch, Kerry pulled out "the ugliest corroded woven-metal ring you've ever seen, which I had bought for a dollar at some metaphysical bookstore." He looked into Dana's eyes and said, "I know this ring isn't much, but I promise that if you say yes, our love will transform it into something much more beautiful. Will you marry me?"

Dana immediately accepted, and Kerry slipped the hideous ring onto her finger. What she didn't know was that he had been practicing his sleight-of-hand skills for days, and as he began to place the awful bauble on her finger, he exchanged it for the real ring. But Dana never looked as he slipped the ring on. (She later admitted to pondering the unpleasant prospect of showing the ring to her friend the next day.) After several minutes, she still hadn't looked. So Kerry mentioned that he had shown the ring to her best friend. Dana looked horrified and exclaimed, "You showed her this?!" She held up her hand — and saw the sparkling one-carat marquise-cut diamond.

Underwater Plane Proposal

Michael and Deanna

*W*hile on Oahu for a friend's wedding, Michael and Deanna went scuba diving at a reef where a World War II-era plane went down. As they were swimming around the remains of the sunken plane 100 feet underwater, their dive master, Lou, caught Deanna's attention. Using sign language, he pointed to a piece of paper stuck in the plane's fuselage and told her to go read it. Deanna ignored his directions repeatedly, figuring it was just some historical literature. (The paper was actually a poem from Michael.) Finally, she swam over to take a look.

While Deanna read the poem, Michael positioned himself behind her and emptied his vest of air so he'd sink to the ocean bottom. Then he got down on his knees and readied the ring. After a while, he started to wonder what was taking her so long. Was she trying to think of a way out of this awkward situation?

In reality, Deanna still hadn't caught on. Her thoughts: "Oh, this is a sweet poem . . . about the pilot?" Finally, it clicked. She turned her head to the right and then quickly to the left. She spotted Lou with the camera and spun around. Deanna was so shocked that all Michael saw were her eyes practically popping out of her mask. Not knowing what to do, she looked to Lou, who motioned "Well, yes or no?" Deanna nodded yes and gave Michael the OK sign.

Telltale Tile

*W*hen David heard that personalized tiles were being sold for the new Seattle Center pavilion, he knew he had found a memorable way to pop the question. He faxed his request for a tile reading: "Amanda, will you marry me? – David." He immediately received a call from a woman who worriedly told him the tiles would not be ready for at least another two months. David told her not to worry, as he didn't even have the ring yet.

When David got the call that the tile was in the ground, his forward thinking almost caused an ulcer. And he quickly went to work on the ring. He took his great-grandmother's turn-of-the-century one-carat stone and had it remounted in a beautiful setting with baguettes and round diamonds.

And then it was time. A quiet, romantic dinner at a nearby Italian restaurant, followed by the idea that they had tickets to "something" at the center, got them to the right location. As they walked beneath trees lit with holiday lights, a saxophonist played a soft tune. David casually suggested that they check out the tiles in the new pavilion. There were some from parents to their kids, kids to their grandparents, friends to friends, and then . . . there was his. David nonchalantly pointed to the tile, saying, "Hey, look at that one." She had to read it a couple of times before it sank in, but she soon realized that it was meant for her.

One-Way Road

Carbon and Erin

Carbon knew how Erin wanted his proposal to go. She wanted a certain kind of ring, she wanted him to ask her father's permission, she wanted him to get down on one knee, and she wanted the proposal to happen at a special place — a place she didn't know about.

So one rainy evening, the couple drove up into the mountains, past a one-lane bridge to a dead-end road. Carbon turned the car around and then stopped in the middle of the bridge. As the couple stood in front of the headlights in the misty rain, Carbon told Erin that since the road was a dead end in one direction, if they wanted to go further in life they could go only one way — the way they were currently facing. He explained that he'd gotten her father's permission. Then he got down on one knee with a ring.

"As we hugged, I told her that I wanted it to be raining so that when we were standing there, we would realize that we could make the best of any weather, and that there will be times in life when we would just have to get wet, accept it and then keep going. Together."

On the way home, Erin asked what was special about the bridge. And he told her, "That was where my father proposed to my mother."

Photo Booth

Russell and Deborah

When it came time for Russell to pop the question, he rented a photo booth and strategically placed it in a nearby park. After a romantic picnic lunch, Russell and Deborah walked hand in hand and "happened upon" the photo booth. He suggested that they get in and take a few pictures. After inspecting the first batch, he told Deborah that he wanted to try again. What she didn't know was that Russell had made a few modifications to his rented booth. He had set up a hidden banner that would drop down behind him when he pulled a special cord. The banner's message? "I love you. Will you marry me?"

Getting back in the photo booth for the retakes, Deborah sat on Russell's lap as he carefully pulled the concealed cord, unveiling the words behind him without her noticing. As they got out, Deborah eagerly waited for the photos to develop. No sooner had they dropped into the slot than she grabbed the photos and looked at their retakes. And looked. And looked. Then smiled and said, "Of course I will."

The photos are now framed and sit on the couple's mantle, said Russell, "a constant reminder of how much we love each other."

Tugging at Her Heartstrings

Graham and Darlene

During a lunch date one afternoon, Graham mentioned reading about a huge tugboat being built nearby that they should go see. He knew where Darlene's heartstrings were — she had long loved watching tugboats from her deck at home. When they got to the tugboat, Graham said he was going to see if he could talk someone into giving them a tour. So he left Darlene, who was dressed in high heels and pearls for an evening at the symphony, and went walking around the tugboat yard.

He came back and reported that the tugboat was scheduled to give a ride to some guy and his son, and the operators had said they could go along. Darlene was used to Graham talking to everyone about everything, so it didn't seem unusual.

The tugboat left its dock and toured the Seattle area's many locks and waterways. The couple spent the ride reminiscing about things they had done together over the years. The captain then announced that they had some extra time and were going to go by the downtown waterfront. As they got closer, Graham took Darlene to the bow of the boat and pointed to something on the shore. While she was searching for what he was pointing at, Graham called her name. Turning around, she was surprised to find him on one knee with a ring.

When the boat docked, there were even more surprises. A stunning black-and-silver '53 Rolls-Royce limo was waiting. After some sightseeing around Seattle and a brief stop on Queen Anne Hill at Kerry Park to look back at their route thus far, they were dropped off at a dock on Lake Union. Graham had chartered a private floatplane to take them to Rosario Resort, in the San Juan Islands, for the weekend.

Seahawks Get Fired Up

Jerry and Tiffany

Tiffany was a cheerleader for the Seattle Seahawks, and both she and Jerry were firefighters. So Jerry figured he'd propose firefighter-style. With the permission of the Seahawks, the Seattle Fire Department and the Seattle Seahawks cheerleaders, Jerry was planning to pop the question during one of the pregame dances that Tiffany was involved in.

He and some fellow firefighters drove two fire trucks in a big parade from Pioneer Square and then walked into the stadium, where the cheerleaders were in the middle of a dance. When they were finished, the announcer started to interview Tiffany, and then introduced the firefighters. All 20 firefighters, in full gear, walked out to meet her. As they approached, Jerry stepped out from the middle of the group, and Tiffany began to cry. In front of both of their families — who had flown in for the occasion — and thousands of screaming fans, Jerry dropped to one knee and "became the luckiest firefighter alive."

♥

Proposal in Pictures

Scott and Stacey

Scott desperately wanted to pop the question to Stacey, but something about being away at Army training was making things a little difficult. So while on a retreat with his comrades, he bought a disposable camera and got creative. He had a pal take several pictures of him holding a sheet of paper. The first said "Stacey." The next said "will." Then "you." Then — well, you get the picture.

He called Stacey and told her he was mailing the camera to her, but that she would have to get the photos developed. He also arranged for his mother to send flowers to Stacey at work on the day she picked up the pictures. With the help of Scott's mother, Stacey sent him his answer — also in the form of pictures. Her piece of paper read "Yes, duh!"

Washington Dinner Train

Erik and Jill

She thought it was just another date night. When they arrived to board the *Spirit of Washington* Dinner Train, Jill was so pleased that Erik had planned the entire evening on his own that she didn't really expect anything more than a good time.

They picked up their tickets and had their picture taken in front of the train, as did all the other passengers. Erik had made reservations to ride in the Mount Rainier Car, one of the observation cars set higher for truly spectacular sightseeing. The couple dined luxuriously by candlelight as the train traveled along the shores of Lake Washington and over the historic Wilburton Trestle. When they arrived at the grounds of Columbia Winery, they toured the winery. Then Erik grabbed Jill's hand and secreted her away. He wasn't finished with his surprise.

It was a foggy, mystical evening. As they walked hand in hand down a dimly lit garden path, they spoke of their love for each other. Then Erik stopped, got down on one knee, and made sure that this "date night" would last forever in both their hearts and memories.

Disguised Surprise

Jason and Alana

*J*ason had the ring, and he wanted to surprise Alana on Christmas morning. So he grabbed several different-sized boxes, each smaller than the next. The largest was a computer box, particularly suitable because Alana wanted a computer for Christmas. To make it all heavy enough to mimic a computer box, Jason included a can of paint, and then wrapped everything up.

At his family's house on Christmas morning, they all opened their gifts, saving the "big one" for last. Everyone knew what was going on, except Alana. Jason went to the tree and started to push the box over to her, staying on his knees the whole time. Then Alana began opening the boxes. When she finally got to the very last one, a small blue box, she looked up at Jason with a surprised smile as he asked her to spend the rest of her life with him.

Photo Album Proposal

Matt and Alison

*H*alfway through a two-week trip to Italy, Matt and Alison were hiking between the five coastal towns of the Cinque Terre. They approached the fourth town, Vernazza, just before sunset. After they had admired the view for a while, Matt turned to Alison and handed her a small photo album containing five pictures. The first was a picture of Matt in Costa Rica in 1999, holding a sign that read "Alison." The second was of him at Whitman College (their alma mater) in 2001 with a sign that said "will." The third, in front of his family's old house in winter 2002, pictured Matt holding a sign that said "you." The fourth, taken outside the couple's apartment, showed him holding the word "marry." The fifth was a picture taken just two days earlier in Florence of him holding a sign that read "me?"

Completely taken by surprise, Alison said, "Of course I will." But Matt wasn't done. "What is the most important thing in the world to you?" he asked her. "My family," responded Alison. And with that, Matt flipped to the back of the album, where he had inserted a card titled "Permission to Propose Marriage." On the card were the signatures of Alison's entire family and her best friend.

♥

Picture Perfect

Blake and Jenna

*B*lake had the ring, he and Jenna had talked about marriage, and he even had her father's permission. The only thing left to do was set a plan in motion — and keep it all a secret from Jenna.

Walking through the student center at his college one day, he saw a display of portraits painted by some art students, several of which were quite good. So he got Jenna to have a photograph taken with him in the "perfect pose" — two profiles, foreheads touching and hands touching each other's faces — she had always wanted for engagement pictures. He told her that he didn't have much money for Valentine's Day and wanted to get it framed for her. What he'd actually done was hire one of the student artists to re-create that very picture, with the engagement ring painted on Jenna's finger. (He was confident.)

During the month and a half it took the artist to finish the painting, Blake convinced Jenna that he had no ring and no money for one and that he hadn't talked to her father yet. When the painting was finally done, he arranged to have it displayed in an art museum. Blake took Jenna to the museum, where they casually looked at the artwork. Eventually, they walked into the room with "the painting," which sat on an easel in the center of the room facing away from them. When Jenna eventually went up to the painting, she looked confused at first. As she walked around the easel looking for a label explaining the painting and the artist, she discovered Blake, down on one knee with a ring.

Up, Up and Away

Grant and Hilary

Grant had always told Hilary that he would never propose on a holiday or a birthday, but instead on a "random Tuesday." And he kept his word.

One random Tuesday, Grant arranged for a friend of Hilary's at work to blindfold her and then lead her down the hall, where she was greeted by familiar hands and a familiar voice. Grant gave Hilary a bouquet, balloons, a plastic lei and a little tiara to wear, and then escorted her to a limousine, where a specially made CD of their favorite songs was playing and a homemade picnic lunch awaited.

Hilary got to take off the blindfold for a while in the limo, but it went back on as they neared their destination. Grant helped her out of the limo and led her to an open field, where Hilary took off her blindfold to find Grant on bended knee with ring in hand — in front of a hot air balloon. A banner attached to the basket read: "Will You Marry Me, Peanut?"

Center Stage

Michael and Elisa

*E*lisa's dream was to someday perform in a musical on Broadway. She loved everything about the stage, from the lights to the theater to the music. It was her passion. So when planning to pop the question, Michael took all this into account.

After going out for dinner one evening, the two returned home to find a "surprise" limo waiting out front. It was the first time they had been in a limo together, and Michael knew that Elisa was trying to figure out what was going on. The limo driver took them to an alley in downtown Seattle, where Michael blindfolded Elisa, then led her through a large back door and onto the stage at the largest musical theater house in Seattle. Two dozen roses surrounded them, and they were illuminated by a single ghost light. Elisa walked back and forth, absorbing the electricity of the stage and the 2,000 empty seats.

Finally, Michael asked her to dance with him. As their song drifted away, he got down on one knee and said, "You know how it's your dream to be on stage? Well, it's my dream to be your husband in the front row . . ."

Rosy Pun

Tom and Amberlyn

One morning, Tom sneaked into Amberlyn's room before she woke up and made a trail of Hershey's Kisses from her bed to the shower. Then he filled the shower with roses. Attached to the roses was the following note: "Now that I have kissed the ground you walk on and showered you with roses, will you marry me?"

Hawaiian Ice

Christian had flown home to Hawaii to introduce
Steph to his family and show her what life in Honolulu was
all about. Today they were on the Big Island to see the lava
flowing from Kilauea into the ocean, quietly enjoying a
three-mile hike along the coastline. At least Christian was.
Steph wasn't a big hiker, and he could tell that she was
getting hot and tired.

Christian stopped and waited for her to get within range
of his voice and said, "Hey, babe, you hot?"

She didn't even make eye contact, responding, "Yeah."

"Do you want some ice?" he asked. That got her attention.

"Yeah," she said. "Did you bring some?"

He pulled out a little black box, dropped to one knee, and
moved the diamond around to get "maximum twinkle" as he
said, "Yeah, I brought some ice."

As she stood there, stunned, all she could manage to say
was "Oh my God. Oh my God."

"My line is 'Will you marry me,' " he continued, "and your
line is . . ."

"Yes," said Steph once, and then again to make sure he
had heard.

116

And the Score Is . . .

Leland and Sharmin

*L*eland had just returned from touring with his band, and Sharmin was in her apartment waiting for him. He walked in at about 10 that night and told Sharmin to make sure they watched the news because he thought something had happened to someone they knew.

Actually, something was going to happen to her. Before returning to the apartment, Leland had contacted a buddy of his who was a sports reporter on a local news show to discuss how he should pop the question. They came up with a pretty good idea.

Leland and Sharmin sat down to watch the broadcast, and the moment arrived. Leland's pal had been cued to report the sports, and he started off by saying, "Tonight we will find out if the Sonics won, if they make the playoffs, and if Sharmin will marry Leland." After a shocked Sharmin said yes, Leland made sure to "call in the results," and his friend soon answered all the viewers' Sonics questions and informed them that yes, Sharmin did say yes.

Photo: Andrew M. Lueck

The Great Pumpkin

Matt and Kirsti

*W*hen they were kids, Matt and Kirsti both enjoyed dressing up as superheroes or vampires and trick-or-treating way past their bedtime. As adults, they spent each Halloween with a bowl of popcorn, watching their favorite Halloween movies. *It's the Great Pumpkin, Charlie Brown* was always at the top of their list.

One Halloween, shortly before midnight, a pickup pulled up to their house and two people dressed in black emerged. Swiftly and silently, they hand-carried dozens of pumpkins into the front yard. Among the pumpkins they placed candles, which cast an eerie glow on the copper jack-o'-lantern rising from the center of the patch.

When the doorbell rang, it was midnight — way too late for trick-or-treaters. Matt jumped up from the couch and raced downstairs with a bowl of candy in hand. As he opened the door, he called to Kirsti to come downstairs. When she came to the door and saw the pumpkin patch that had sprung up, a look of bewilderment and delight came over her face. A bit dazed, she carefully plucked the copper jack-o'-lantern from the middle of the patch, and found a ring inside.

Opposites Attract

Brian and Ann

*B*rian, an Army finance officer, was analytical and "by the book." He made a detailed plan before any action, and always had a backup plan or two. Ann, on the other hand, is more spontaneous. When the couple went on vacation, Brian developed complex spreadsheets detailing every move; Ann took pictures and made scrapbooks.

Ann wasn't surprised when Brian took a pragmatic approach to their future. Before they were officially engaged, the couple had most of the wedding details planned. Brian even comparison shopped for the ring and put together a spreadsheet so she could choose the perfect ring. After she'd made her choice, the waiting began. And the longer she waited, the more she wondered. He knew the answer, but she wanted a special and unique proposal.

The evening before her birthday, they both stayed up reading, and he pointed out that since it was after midnight, it was officially her birthday and she should open her presents. After she did, he said he had one more gift. He had made her a scrapbook. Ann was so impressed by his creative gift that it took her a few minutes to realize what was inside; she was too busy looking at the pictures and reading the things he'd written.

"It was the perfect combination of the two of us, full of photos of our travels together, and even a spreadsheet with this math problem: If 1 + 1 = 2, can 2 = 1?" The answer was on the final page — Two can't equal One unless the Two become One — along with her ring and the question she'd been waiting for.

120

The Helicopter Proposal

Casey and Noelle

Casey knew the question, was pretty sure he knew the answer, and also knew the perfect mountaintop location. "I spent much of my childhood years camping, hunting and exploring the terrain by motorbike," he said. From the top of the mountain, they'd be able to see everything: from Seattle skyscrapers all the way to the San Juan Islands and the Olympic Mountains in between. The only thing left to figure out was how to get Noelle there without spoiling the surprise. So Casey, an experienced helicopter pilot, invited her to join him on a flight to Eastern Washington, where he'd be working for several weeks. She didn't suspect a thing.

As they approached the mountain, Casey told Noelle that the helicopter was having some electrical problems. What?! Noelle kept her cool. They landed, and Casey pretended to work on the electrical system, located just behind her seat. After a few seconds, he announced that he had found the problem. Noelle unbuckled so she could see for herself, while Casey pulled out the ring and got down on one knee.

When Noelle turned around, she expected wiring and tools — and got a sparkling diamond engagement ring instead. But she quickly screamed "Yes!" and the couple celebrated with sparkling cider as the sun set on a perfect proposal.

Knight in
Shining Armor

Chris and Sarah

Once upon a time, a well-meaning young man attempted a grand gesture of chivalry and romance. Aspiring to be a knight in shining armor, Chris donned 84 pounds of head-to-toe metal, a cape and a sword — and tried to ride a horse to his lady fair.

Off he rode to find his girlfriend, Sarah, who was working with her students and their horses in the arena. Gaining confidence as he rode, Chris gave the horse a little cluck and kick to get it to walk a bit faster. The horse began to pick up speed, and so did the noise from the armor. The more noise the armor made, the faster the horse went. Chris couldn't see and he couldn't stop. And as he went galloping blindly into the arena, the clanking started to spook the other horses. Pandemonium ensued. Chris's horse did eventually stop at a fence — stop, rear up and throw him off, that is.

Sarah, the intended object of his attentions, was unaware of what was really happening. Lying on the ground, Chris had no idea how to regain his "severe loss of cool." Someone soon informed Sarah that the mound of metal on the ground was her boyfriend, and she quickly realized that this crazy display of chivalry was likely part of a proposal plan.

In the end, Chris's injuries were minor — except those to his ego — and they lived happily ever after.

Soda Popping the Question

John and Jessica

Photos: Kathryn Aguilo

*I*t was their fourth anniversary as a couple, and John suggested that they celebrate with a trip down memory lane. So they headed for their favorite beachside park and took a leisurely walk around the U-shaped dock where they had meandered so many times before. They checked out a much-loved view of Seattle and other familiar sites. They even peered into the murky water to see if anything was swimming below.

It was cold, so they soon returned to the park's sandy beach, where out of the blue, John pointed to an old bottle partially buried in the sand. He urged Jessica to take a look, but she didn't understand why he would want her to check out an old bottle that could be covered with who-knows-what. Subtle hints weren't changing her mind, so John picked up the bottle and showed it to her. When Jessica saw the customized Jones Soda Berry Lemonade bottle — with a picture of her and John on the label — she realized this wasn't just any beach-strewn bottle.

John turned the bottle over to reveal a special message on the back. Four capitalized words immediately caught Jessica's eye. Her heart raced as she read the whole message: "Jessica, you are the most beautiful and caring person that I know. I love you with all my heart and I want to be with you forever. Will You Marry Me? Love, Johnny." Jessica said she "felt like we were in a movie" as John then pulled a ring box out of his jacket pocket, got down on one knee and popped the question.

Beach House

Hani and Danielle

A surprise was waiting for her downtown, Hani told Danielle one sunny Saturday morning. Then he handed her three mysterious envelopes, asking her to open the first after she'd parked the car. The first envelope contained the word "will" and directed her to a luxurious manicure appointment. Afterward, she opened the second envelope, which contained the word "you" and sent her off for a relaxing body wrap. After an enjoyable morning of pampering, Danielle opened the third envelope. This one contained the word "marry" and sent her back to the house.

On the outside of Hani's door was another envelope. And on the other side of the door was Hani, standing in his living room. One hundred pounds of sand covered the floor (on a plastic tarp). Scattered over the sand were numerous pieces of sand glass, starfish and seashells.

Hani had originally planned for this moment to take place at a beach near a romantic bed-and-breakfast, but he hadn't been able to persuade Danielle to squeeze such a getaway into their packed schedules — so he did the next best thing. And Danielle didn't seem to mind. She dreamily entered Hani's re-creation of the Washington coast with her fourth and final envelope, which contained the word "me," and happily accepted his beachside proposal.

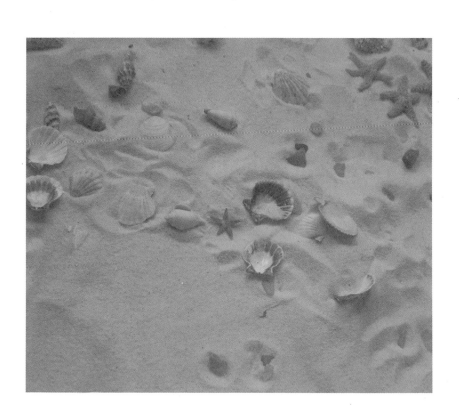

Proposal Noir

Norilyn thought they were going to see a short film that one of Jay's clients had produced. When they got to the theater, the client greeted them and told them to have a seat.

"Where is everyone?" Norilyn asked as they sat down in the empty theater. "I'll feel bad if nobody shows up."

Jay said he'd find out what was going on. As he left, the lights dimmed, the screen lit up and familiar music began to play. On the screen, something else familiar appeared — the couple's scrapbook. Jay had put together a kind of movie scrapbook with memorabilia that he'd collected over the years from things they'd done, places they'd been, music they'd listened to and notes they'd shared.

At the end of the film, Jay's hand appeared on the screen and turned the page of their scrapbook to a blank sheet. He then proceeded to write the words "Will you marry me?" across the screen. The screen faded to white. And Jay walked back into the room to ask Norilyn the big question.

Honor Thy Father

Benson and Jamie

At 44, Jamie had pretty much decided that she just wasn't destined to experience "real love" the way she'd envisioned. So what did she have to lose by posting her profile on a Jewish dating service? A short time later, she received a note that led to a month of written exchanges, a creative first phone call, some detective work and, finally, an unpretentious walk around Green Lake with their dogs as chaperones. There was chemistry. There was depth. There were shared values. It was just the way Jamie had always imagined it. And she knew that a proposal was coming — she'd helped pick out the ring — but she had no idea when or how.

One day, during a romantic lunch complete with French Champagne, Jamie presented Benson with a pair of her father's cuff links, expecting a ring in return. But Benson had other ideas. The couple left the restaurant and drove to the cemetery where her father was buried. Jamie had always dreamed of her father walking her down the aisle. But those little-girl dreams had faded when her father died tragically more than 10 years before her special someone came along. Standing at the graveside that afternoon, Benson told Jamie's father how much he loved her and asked for his blessing. With tears streaming down his face, Benson then turned to Jamie and asked if she would marry him.

Toying with Her Affections

Brian and Marilyn

Brian and Marilyn were both big *Star Wars* fans, so when a FedEx package from Toys "R" Us showed up at work with a long-awaited Darth Tater toy (think evil Potato Head), she was excited. Her boyfriend just happened to be there when the package arrived, so the two went back to her desk to check it out. She opened the package, examined the plastic toy with its specially marketed accessories, and noticed that it was missing its arm and cape.

"I wonder where the other parts are?" Brian said. Marilyn thought they were probably in the rear compartment, where the spare parts were kept. Brian encouraged her to check, so she opened the sealed package and peered into the storage compartment — where she did not find spare parts. What she did find was a velvet ring box with an enameled titanium ring that read "Use the Force." A note inside said, "I can see you now, walking down to the Imperial Death March. The only question is, will you 'use the force' and marry me?"

♥

The Perfect Dish

Kevin and Kate

One long weekend, Kevin invited Kate on a romantic trip to Victoria, British Columbia. Arriving at their hotel, they were told that their room had "plumbing problems" and were given a complimentary upgrade to a suite, the same one the Queen of England had used during her stay in Victoria.

The couple spent the day shopping, and Kevin suggested they look at engagement rings. Since Kate figured this meant he hadn't bought a ring yet, she put any thoughts of a proposal during this perfect weekend out of her mind. They looked through rings until Kevin was satisfied that he knew what Kate liked. "White gold, diamond in the middle, and little diamonds on either side," he kept saying. And then they went back to the hotel for a nice dinner.

As they were sipping their wine, the waiter came over with a covered dish and said, "I told our chef you were visiting from Seattle, and he has sent a little treat for you." The waiter lifted the cover off, and there was the ring — white gold, diamond in the middle, and little diamonds on either side — sitting on an oyster shell surrounded by orchids. Then Kevin got down on one knee and proposed in front of everyone in the restaurant.

The Proposer

Larry and Heidi

Photo: Bootsy Holler

*H*eidi thought she and Larry were having dinner with friends at Six Seven, in Seattle's Edgewater Hotel. But their friends had called while they were en route to the restaurant to say they'd have to cancel because their kids were sick. Heidi never suspected that a secret plan had been set in motion. She and Larry enjoyed a romantic dinner, lingered over dessert and had a lovely time.

Outside the restaurant, the commotion was just beginning as a smoke-gray 1959 Cadillac limo pulled up to the building. Out stepped a tall, handsome man sporting a black suit, black T-shirt and black hat, the kind of guy you couldn't miss if you tried. Handcuffed to his wrist was a sleek steel briefcase. By now, the other restaurant patrons had figured out that something was up, but Heidi was still blissfully clueless. As "The Proposer" — a complimentary service offered by E.E. Robbins, Seattle's Engagement Ring Store — approached Larry and Heidi's table, every pair of eyes in the restaurant was following the tall, handsome mystery man. So was a cameraman from the local television show *Evening Magazine*. Larry had given the show permission to film the proposal for a Valentine's Day special.

The 6-foot-5 gentleman walked slowly over to the couple and placed the briefcase on their table. He proceeded to unlock the handcuff and the steel case, and then pulled out a beautiful blue ring box. Handing the box to Larry, he announced, "Here is your delivery, sir." And then he left. The striking man in black may have been the center of attention when he entered the room, but as he departed, all eyes were on Heidi as she gave a resounding "Yes!"

Cinderella Story

Corey and Holly

*I*t was just Holly, her mom and her sister. They were out for a special night to see the ballet *Cinderella*, where they had front row, balcony box seats. As Act I came to a close, an usher approached and asked if she was Holly. When she said yes, he handed her a box and made a quick exit.

The lights were still down, and it was difficult to see. Holly looked at her mother, but she just gave her daughter a silly grin. Intrigued, Holly tugged at the ribbon. As her eyes began to adjust, she finally managed to open the box, and a beautiful aroma came billowing out from a bed of potpourri. Placed ever so perfectly on this cushion of dried flowers was a sparkling crystal glass slipper holding a tiny note card, where the word "Cinderella" was written ever so neatly. Her hands shaking, Holly opened the card, which read, "Merry Me!" (misspelled, but she knew what it meant).

As the lights came up and the crowd watched, Holly turned to see her boyfriend, Corey — "the most handsome of princes" — in his tuxedo and white gloves. His arms were full of roses, and he held a little black box with "a ring of the most brilliant of diamonds."

Fishing for an Answer

Chad and Kelli

*C*had's girlfriend had never been on a fishing trip. He planned to remedy that, and fish for an answer while he was at it. Out on the dock with their poles in the water, Chad told Kelli to reel in her line so that he could rebait her hook. But then he suddenly "remembered" that he'd forgotten the bait, and asked her to go get it from the car.

While she was gone, he took out the engagement ring, tied it tightly to the end of the pole and then tossed the line lightly into the water. When Kelli returned, Chad said that he'd found some bait. After a while, he told her to reel in the line — and up came the ring. Chad got down on his knee and told Kelli that she'd captured his heart.

Champagne Kisses
in the Snow

Keith and Aimee

A day before his planned proposal, Keith took the day off and went up to the Carbon River entrance to Mount Rainier to find the perfect spot and make preparations. He found a long rock bar in the middle of the river, with a view of some mountains and the peak of Mount Rainier. He cleared the snow off a small area and spelled out "Will You Marry Me Aimee" with rocks, then covered it with hemlock branches to protect it from falling fluff. Lastly, Keith stashed a bottle of champagne in the river and headed home, picking up 14 pink roses along the way, which he hid in his car.

The next day he took Aimee out to the river. It was snowing heavily, a beautiful sight. Keith brushed some snow off the hemlock branches he'd arranged the day before and said, "Wow, take a look at this — does that say something?" Aimee, who thought he had just been clearing a spot to sit, soon realized what the rocks spelled out and began to cry. Keith got down on one knee, showed her the engagement ring and repeated the question she'd just read. After an enthusiastic "Yes! Yes! I'm so happy!" from Aimee, Keith led her over to the river and pulled the champagne out of the water, brought out some champagne flutes from his backpack, and gave her a bouquet of roses.

The couple then hiked through the snow to a beautiful waterfall. "The trees were laden with snow, everything was covered in white, and the waterfall made a beautiful setting for a celebration kiss," Keith said.

Acknowledgments

*I*t's no mystery that writing and publishing a book is truly a collaborative effort that would not be possible without a lot of help from a lot of great people. On that note, I would like to first thank our wonderful writer, Alicia M. Lawver, who helped write each one of the 99 proposal stories in our book while being fully committed to maintaining the integrity of every couple's own words about their true-life proposals. I would like to express my appreciation as well to Judy Gouldthorpe, our copy editor, who fine-tuned all of our stories.

I would also like to thank my good friend Erik Hall, an amazingly talented artist who honored us by painting a four-by-five-foot masterpiece that now hangs in our Belltown store and which serves as the cover for our book.

A thousand thanks to Wilson Public Relations, and specifically to the dedicated and hardworking Nathan Hambley. Nathan spent countless hours contacting each of the couples, helping to assemble all of the creative and romantic proposal stories included in our book, and coordinating a thousand and one details. My sincere thanks also to Lauren Fior for her efficiency and efforts in helping to launch our book.

And last but certainly not least, I would further like to extend my heartfelt appreciation to our kind and creative publishers, Jody Ericson Dorow and Nancy Gellos. With their professional guidance and gracious personas, they helped make the publishing process surprisingly painless and amazingly enjoyable.

Emerson Robbins

Emerson Robbins has deep roots in the Pacific Northwest as well as the engagement ring business. His grandfather's store, Ben Tipp Diamonds in downtown Seattle, was the region's leading purveyor of diamonds from the 1920s to the 1950s.

Born in Seattle, Emerson relocated to Southern California, where he and his brother Steve founded the nation's first chain of stores dedicated solely to wedding and engagement rings. Robbins Bros. is now the *World's Biggest Engagement Ring Store*, with locations across the country.

In 1998, Emerson happily returned to Seattle and soon after opened the first E.E. Robbins — named for his father — on the corner of First Avenue and Blanchard, in the heart of Belltown and just a few blocks from where his grandfather's store had been. Now with several stores in the Seattle area, E.E. Robbins has become the premier engagement and wedding ring store in the Pacific Northwest.

Emerson's passion for his life's work comes from a true sense of romance, inspired by his own parents and his wife, Sherri. As he often says, "Love may not make the world go 'round, but it sure makes the ride more enjoyable."

Alicia M. Lawver

Alicia Manley Lawver is a freelance writer who has
worked for several Northwest publications, including
*The Bridal Connection, Northwest Women's Journal, WAC
Magazine, The Daily World* (Aberdeen), *The Olympian*
and *The Peninsula Gateway.*

Alicia's writing career stretches back to her childhood
days on a farm in Oregon's Willamette Valley. She met
her husband, Nathaniel, on the first day of classes at Pacific
Lutheran University, in Tacoma, Washington. Two and
a half years later, he arranged a romantic getaway to
Lake Quinault without raising a single suspicion. After
an adventure-filled road trip to the remote destination, the
couple sat down for a lovely dinner at the lodge's restaurant.
They ate, they talked, they laughed. As the meal began
to wind down, the waitress brought over a little something
extra: embossed scrolls bearing love poems, a bouquet
of roses — and a little box. A decade later, they're living
happily ever after with their three young children in Tacoma.

Erik Hall

Photo: Kevin Clark

Erik Hall was born in Portland, Oregon, and grew up
in a military family that moved frequently. He returned
to the Northwest in recent years, seeking a sense of
community with friends, art and business.

"A landscape by definition is an expanse of scenery,"
he says. "This expanse seems infinite to me. My work
is largely an exploration of color, the adjustment of shapes,
and the tolerance of the two in concert with one another,
whether they are man-made or natural."

Erik is entirely self-taught. His work has been displayed
at a number of art galleries, businesses and public spaces.

"True love stories never have endings."

- Richard Bach

Photo: Bootsy Holler